50 AMERICAN REVOLUTIONS
YOU'RE NOT SUPPOSED TO KNOW

Reclaiming American Patriotism

by Mickey Z

disinformation

Published by The Disinformation Company Ltd.
163 Third Avenue, Suite 108, New York, NY 10003 / Tel.: +1.212.691.1605 / Fax: +1.212.691.1606
www.disinfo.com

Design & Layout: Rebecca Meek

Library of Congress Control Number: 2005926122

ISBN-13: 978-1-932857-23-8

ISBN-10: 1-932857-23-0

Printed in the USA

Distributed in the USA and Canada by: Consortium Book Sales and Distribution
1045 Westgate Drive, Suite 90, St Paul, MN 55114 / Toll Free: +1.800.283.3572 / Local: +1.651.221.9035 / Fax: +1.651.221.0124 / www.cbsd.com

Attention colleges and universities, corporations and other organizations:
Quantity discounts are available on bulk purchases of this book for educational training purposes, fund-raising, or gift-giving. Special books, booklets, or book excerpts can also be created to fit your specific needs. For information contact the Marketing Department of The Disinformation Company Ltd.

50 AMERICAN REVOLUTIONS YOU'RE NOT SUPPOSED TO KNOW

Reclaiming American Patriotism

by Mickey Z

The lover of a subversive is also a subversive.
— Martin Espada

The tree of liberty must be refreshed from time to time with the blood of patriots and tyrants.
— Thomas Jefferson

I've never seen one history book that tells me how anybody feels.
— Bob Dylan

CONTENTS

CONTENTS

INTRODUCTION

Patriot Acts
Employing weapons of mass instruction

We have two American flags always: one for the rich and one for the poor. When the rich fly, it means that things are under control; when the poor fly, it means danger, revolution, anarchy.
— **Henry Miller**

They're hoping soon my kind will drop and die / But I'm gonna wave my freak flag high.
— **Jimi Hendrix, "If 6 Was 9"**

My wife Michele and I went to the Yankee game on May Day 2004. They gave out free caps: "NY" on the front, of course… and a shiny patch on the back of the hat acknowledged the giveaway day sponsor: Hess.

The House that Ruth Built became a moveable ad for oil (instant replays brought to you by Dodge).

The seventh inning stretch required fans to stand in honor of the "men and women in uniform" who fight to "preserve our way of life." Fifty thousand removed their free caps, watched a digitized flag wave on the big screen, and held the Hess patch over cholesterol-laden hearts while belting out "God Bless America," collectively choosing to ignore the blood being spilled to keep the world safe for petroleum.

The Yankees won (as usual) and many of those fans promptly rushed out to drive home in their ubiquitous SUVs… adorned, of course, with the ubiquitous "support the troops" yellow ribbon sticker.

Surely I wasn't the only one contemplating this "my country right or wrong" concept of patriotism… but just as surely, if I had articulated those feelings, some of my fellow Yankee fans would have responded with hostility.

I know this from experience. For example, when I wrote an article about Pat Tillman that was critical of the hero worship upon his death, many patriots sent e-mails that voiced sentiments like this: "What really sickens me is that good people like Pat died so you can talk shit about him."

It seems what offends this breed of patriot most is when someone else actually exercises the freedom they claim to adore.

To such folks, says author Michael Parenti, "America is a simplified ideological abstraction, an emotive symbol represented by other abstract symbols like the flag. It is the object of a faithlike devotion, unencumbered by honest history." For them, Parenti adds, "those who do not share in this uncritical Americanism ought to go live in some other country."

From taking up arms against one's oppressor to using art and words as weapons of mass instruction, the 50 episodes presented here celebrate a different form of patriotism… one based on challenging tradition and taking action. Whether inspired by personal conviction or a larger social ambition, those featured herein chose the more difficult, non-conformist path. In a society as heavily conditioned as ours, I submit such a choice is, in and of itself, a revolutionary act.

Radical historian Howard Zinn tells us that a revolution is "an endless succession of surprises, moving zigzag toward a more decent society." He explains: "We don't have to engage in grand, heroic actions to participate in the process of change. Small acts, when multiplied by millions of people, can transform the world."

Patriot acts, if you will.

Noted zigzagger Ani DiFranco sings, "Beneath the good and the kind and the stupid and the cruel, there's a fire just waiting for fuel."

Consider this book my contribution of renewable energy… ⛌

01
THOMAS PAINE ADDS FUEL TO THE REVOLUTIONARY FIRE

We are often told actions speak louder than words but the life of Thomas Paine (1737-1809) tells a different story. Born in England, Paine found a home as resident radical in the Colonies… his words inspiring a nation to independence. *Common Sense*, written anonymously as a pamphlet in January 1776 and read by every member of Congress, sold roughly 500,000 copies. (To perform a similar feat today, an author would have to sell more than 46 million books.) It stirred the spirits of colonial America by putting into words what those seeking freedom from British rule had been feeling for a long, long time.

Viewed through the prism of the twenty-first century, *Common Sense* reads, at times, like something one might hear at a hokey school play:

O ye that love mankind! Ye that dare oppose, not only the tyranny, but the tyrant, stand forth! Every spot of the old world is overrun with oppression. Freedom hath been hunted round the globe. Asia, and Africa, have long expelled her. Europe regards her like a stranger, and England hath given her warning to depart. O! receive the fugitive, and prepare in time an asylum for mind.

But, dated vernacular aside, Paine does make clear what he is trying to provoke, e.g. "I have never met with a man, either in England or America, who hath not confessed his opinion, that a separation between the countries, would take place one time or other. And there is no instance in which we have shown less judgment, than in endeavoring to describe, what we call, the ripeness or fitness of the Continent for independence."

Common Sense popularized the concept that even a good government is, at best, a necessary evil. Paine effectively demonized King George III and argued against a small island nation like England ruling a continent on the other side of the ocean. Perhaps most importantly, *Common Sense* painted a post-independence picture of peace and prosperity. More so than the battles at Lexington and Concord, which preceded the release of Paine's influential pamphlet, it was *Common Sense* that served as the spark to light the revolutionary flame.

Even though Paine, denounced as a drunken atheist, died in poverty, his legacy remains secure. *Common Sense* is the precursor to all revolutionary manifestoes. ☿

TIMELINE:
March 31, 1776: Abigail Adams writes her husband John: "Remember, all men would be tyrants if they could. If particular care and attention is not paid to the Ladies, we are determined to foment a Rebellion, and will not hold ourselves bound by any laws by which we have no voice or Representation."
September 3, 1783: The Treaty of Paris is signed, formally ending the war for independence.

02
THE BILL OF RIGHTS

Amendments 1-10 of the Constitution: Ratified on December 15, 1791

The Conventions of a number of the States having, at the time of adopting the Constitution, expressed a desire, in order to prevent misconstruction or abuse of its powers, that further declaratory and restrictive clauses should be added, and as extending the ground of public confidence in the Government will best insure the beneficent ends of its institution;

Resolved, by the Senate and House of Representatives of the United States of America, in Congress assembled, two-thirds of both Houses concurring, that the following articles be proposed to the Legislatures of the several States, as amendments to the Constitution of the United States; all or any of which articles, when ratified by three-fourths of the said Legislatures, to be valid to all intents and purposes as part of the said Constitution, namely:

Amendment I: Congress shall make no law respecting an establishment of religion, or prohibiting the free exercise thereof; or abridging the freedom of speech, or of the press; or the right of the people peaceably to assemble, and to petition the government for a redress of grievances.

Amendment II: A well regulated militia, being necessary to the security of a free state, the right of the people to keep and bear arms, shall not be infringed.

Amendment III: No soldier shall, in time of peace be quartered in any house, without the consent of the owner, nor in time of war, but in a manner to be prescribed by law.

Amendment IV: The right of the people to be secure in their persons, houses, papers, and effects, against unreasonable searches and seizures, shall not be violated, and no warrants shall issue, but upon probable cause, supported by oath or affirmation, and particularly describing the place to be searched, and the persons or things to be seized.

Amendment V: No person shall be held to answer for a capital, or otherwise infamous crime, unless on a presentment or indictment of a grand jury, except in cases arising in the land or naval forces, or in the militia, when in actual service in time of war or public danger; nor shall any person be subject for the same offense to be twice put in jeopardy of life or limb; nor shall be compelled in any criminal case to be a witness against himself, nor be deprived of life, liberty, or property, without due process of law; nor shall private property be taken for public use, without just compensation.

Amendment VI: In all criminal prosecutions, the accused shall enjoy the right to a speedy and public trial, by an impartial jury of the state and district wherein the crime shall have been committed, which district shall have been previously ascertained by law, and to be informed of the nature and cause of the accusation; to be confronted with the witnesses against him; to have compulsory process for obtaining witnesses in his favor, and to have the assistance of counsel for his defense.

Amendment VII: In suits at common law, where the value in controversy shall exceed twenty dollars, the right of trial by jury shall be preserved, and no fact tried by a jury, shall be otherwise reexamined in any court of the United States, than according to the rules of the common law.

Amendment VIII: Excessive bail shall not be required, nor excessive fines imposed, nor cruel and unusual punishments inflicted.

Amendment IX: The enumeration in the Constitution, of certain rights, shall not be construed to deny or disparage others retained by the people.

Amendment X: The powers not delegated to the United States by the Constitution, nor prohibited by it to the states, are reserved to the states respectively, or to the people. ▯

TIMELINE:
June 11, 1776: Congress appoints a committee to compose a declaration of independence.
1783: Noting the Bill of Rights proclamation that "all men are created equal," the Massachusetts Supreme Court outlaws slavery in that state.

03
SHAYS REBELLION

Long before the cries of "support the troops" became commonplace during every U.S. military intervention, the powers-that-be made it clear how much they intended to follow their own advice.

"When Massachusetts passed a state constitution in 1780, it found few friends among the poor and middle class, many of them veterans from the Continental Army still waiting for promised bonuses," explains historian Kenneth C. Davis. To add to this, excessive property taxes were combined with polling taxes designed to prevent the poor from voting. "No one could hold state office without being quite wealthy," Howard Zinn adds. "Furthermore, the legislature was refusing to issue paper money, as had been done in some other states, like Rhode Island, to make it easier for debt-ridden farmers to pay off their creditors."

Perhaps heeding the advice of Thomas Jefferson that "a little rebellion" is necessary, Massachusetts farmers fought back when their property was seized due to lack of debt repayment. Armed and organized, their ranks grew into the hundreds. Local sheriffs called out the militia… but the militia sided with the farmers. The Supreme Judicial Court of Massachusetts indicted eleven members of the rebellion. Those who had so recently fomented revolt were no longer tolerant of such insurrection.

Enter Daniel Shays (1747-1825): Massachusetts farmer and former Army captain. He chose not to stand by idly as battle lines were being drawn and friends of his faced imprisonment. In September 1786, Shays led an army of some 700 farmers, workers, and veterans into Springfield. "Onetime radical Sam Adams, now part of the Boston Establishment, drew up a Riot Act," says Davis, "allowing the authorities to jail anyone without a trial." Shays' army swelled to more than 1000 men.

Writing from Paris, Jefferson offered tacit approval for, at least, the concept of rebellion. Closer to home, the American aristocracy was less than pleased. Sam Adams again: "In monarchy, the crime of treason may admit of being pardoned or lightly punished, but the man who dares rebel against the laws of a republic ought to suffer death."

In a classic shape-of-things-to-come scenario, Boston merchants pooled money to raise an army to be led by General Benjamin Lincoln, one of George Washington's war commanders. Clashes were fierce but the outnumbered rebels were on the run by winter. Most were killed or captured. Some were hanged while others, including Shays, were eventually pardoned in 1787.

Shays died in poverty and obscurity but the rebellion he helped lead not only served as an example of radical patriotism, it resulted in some concrete reforms including, as Davis states, "the end of direct taxation, lowered court costs, and the exemption of workmen's tools and household necessities from the debt process." ⛉

TIMELINE:
1788: Mercy Otia Warren is the only woman to take part in the public debate over the proposed Constitution. She called it a "many-headed monster."
1794: Pennsylvania farmers revolt against a whiskey tax. George Washington rides out with 13,000 men to put down the rebellion.

04
NAT TURNER PUTS THE SOUTH ON NOTICE

Nothing struck deeper fear into the hearts of southerners, whether they held slaves or not, than the idea of a slave revolt.
— **Historian Kenneth C. Davis**

Two earlier slave revolts — by Gabriel Prosser and Denmark Vesey — had blazed the path and shattered the myth of African slaves as docile co-conspirators in their plight… but it was Nat Turner (1800-1831) who brought reality into the homes of Southerners. Born in Southampton County, Virginia, the deeply religious Turner was prone to visions and dubbed "The Prophet" by his fellow slaves.

As a young man, Turner was sold to Thomas Moore. Upon Moore's death, Turner moved to the home of Joseph Travis, the new husband of Moore's widow. In each setting, he was remembered for his praying, fasting, and visions.

A solar eclipse in February 1831 was interpreted by Turner to be the sign for him to take action. He and a few trusted friends commenced planning an insurrection. Originally slated for July 4 but postponed due to Turner being ill, the plan resurfaced on August 13, when an atmospheric disturbance made the sun appear bluish-green. Again construing this as a sign, Turner and his fellow slaves decided to act. On August 21, they

THE
CONFESSIONS
OF
NAT TURNER,
THE LEADER
OF
**THE LATE INSURRECTION
IN SOUTHAMPTON, VA.**

AS FULLY AND VOLUNTARILY MADE TO
THOMAS R. GRAY,

In the prison where he was confined, and acknowledged by him to be ... when read to him the Court of Southampton; with the certificate, under seal of the Court convened at Jerusalem, Nov. 5, 1831, for his trial.

ALSO,
AN AUTHENTIC ACCOUNT
OF THE
WHOLE INSURRECTION,
WITH
Lists of the Whites who were Murdered,
AND OF THE
Negroes brought before the Court of Southampton, and there sentenced, &c.

RICHMOND:
PUBLISHED BY THOMAS R. GRAY.
T. W. WHITE, PRINTER.

1832.

...YOU'RE NOT
SUPPOSED TO KNOW

killed the entire Travis family as they slept. Thus began a house-to-house murdering spree that swelled Turner's "army" to more than 40 slaves. By the morning of August 22, word of the rebellion had gotten out… prompting a calling up of the militia and a wave of fright through the region. Turner and his men continued marching and killing but were badly outnumbered by the white militia. Many slaves were arrested or killed, but Turner eluded capture for two months.

"The whites around Southampton… were thrown into an utter panic, many of them fleeing the state," says Davis.

By the time Turner was finally caught on October 30, 55 whites had been stabbed, shot, and clubbed to death. Turner's actions, while doomed to end with his death at the hands of the state, had impacted the South and its "peculiar institution" in a permanent manner.

As Davis explains, "To whites and slaves alike, he had acquired some mystical qualities that made him larger than life, and even after his hanging, slave owners feared his influence."

Turner and 54 others were executed but the rebellion brought Virginia to the verge of abolishing slavery. The state chose instead to clamp down harder on slaves but this served only to heighten awareness of how untenable the situation had become. In the immediate future lurked John Brown, the Underground Railroad, Frederick Douglass, *The Liberator*, and, of course, the Emancipation Proclamation.

The South had indeed been put on notice.

Postscript:

William Styron's 1968 novel, *The Confessions of Nat Turner*, was awarded a Pulitzer Prize.

TIMELINE:

1808: Slave importation is outlawed.

1820: Women's rights advocate Susan B. Anthony is born.

1828: The Cherokee Legislative Council begins publishing the *Cherokee Phoenix*, a newspaper in both English and Cherokee.

1830: Mary Harris "Mother" Jones is born. The lifetime agitator was known to say: "I'm not a humanitarian. I'm a hell-raiser."

05
THE SEMINOLE–AFRICAN ALLIANCE

The Native American Indian people that comprised the Seminole Nation grew out of the Creek Nation in Florida. Multilingual and diverse, the Seminoles (from a word meaning "runaway") became infamous for intermingling with runaway slaves from Georgia and the Carolinas… slaves that, as historian William Loren Katz explains, "Since 1738 had built prosperous, free, self-governing communities."

Katz explains the genesis of this alliance: "Africans began to instruct Seminoles in methods of rice cultivation they had learned in Senegambia and Sierra Leone. Then the two peoples forged an agricultural and military alliance that challenged slave-hunters and then U.S. troops. Some African families lived in separate villages, others married Seminoles, and the two peoples with a common foe shaped joint diplomatic and military initiatives. Africans, with the most to lose, rose to Seminole leadership as warriors, interpreters, and military advisors."

"The two races, the negro and the Indian, are rapidly approximating; they are identical in interests and feelings," said U.S. Major General Sidney Thomas Jesup at the time. "Should the Indians remain in this territory the negroes among them will form a rallying point for runaway negroes from the adjacent states; and if they remove, the fastness of the country will be immediately occupied by negroes."

What Katz calls "the first foreign invasion launched by the new U.S. government" was the 1816 assault on the Seminole Nation… an assault met with fierce resistance. After Spain sold Florida to the U.S. in 1819, America's full military might was put to work reclaiming the land from both former slaves and their indigenous co-inhabitants. In a scenario that would presage future U.S. interventions in the Philippines, Vietnam, and Iraq, roughly 4,000 black and Indian fighters effectively utilized hit-and-run guerrilla tactics against more than 200,000 U.S. Army troops.

"Because they fought on their own soil, Seminole forces ran circles around the numerically and technologically superior U.S. armies," Katz says. "U.S. officers violated agreements, destroyed crops, cattle and horses, and seized women and children as hostages. They tried to racially divide the Seminole Nation. Nothing worked and resistance only stiffened."

Although the sheer numbers would eventually bring defeat to the brave Red and Black Seminoles, the resistance of Christmas Eve 1837 remains a powerful example of the cunning forces of right prevailing over the arrogant power of might.

"An estimated 380 to 480 freedom-fighting African and Indian members of the Seminole nation threw back an advance of more than a thousand U.S. Army and other troops led by Colonel Zachary Taylor, a future president of the United States," says Katz. "The Seminoles so badly mauled the invaders that Taylor ordered his soldiers to fall back, bury their dead, tend to their wounded and ponder the largest single U.S. defeat in decades of Indian warfare. The battle of Lake Okeechobee is not a story you will find in school or college textbooks, and has slipped from the public consciousness. But in a country that cherishes its freedom-fighting heritage, Black and Red Seminoles of Florida sent everyone a message that deserves to be remembered and honored." ⛢

TIMELINE:
1831: Publication of the first issue of William Lloyd Garrison's abolitionist journal, *The Liberator*.
1840: Harriet Tubman (1820-1913) helps start the Underground Railroad to guide slaves to freedom.
1841: Former slave Frederick Douglass (1817-1895) delivers his first anti-slavery speech.

Patriot Words...
I can train a monkey to wave an American flag. That does not make the monkey patriotic.
— **Scott Ritter, former UN weapons inspector in Iraq**

06
LOWELL MILL GIRLS GET ORGANIZED

In vain do I try to soar in fancy and imagination above
the dull reality around me but beyond the roof of the factory I cannot rise.

— **Anonymous Lowell Mill worker, 1826**

Lowell, Massachusetts was named after the wealthy Lowell family. They owned numerous textile mills, which attracted the unmarried daughters of New England farmers. These young girls worked in the mills and lived in supervised dormitories. On average, a Lowell Mill Girl worked for three years before leaving to marry. Living and working together often forged a camaraderie that would later find an unexpected outlet.

What had the potential to become a relatively agreeable system for all involved was predictably exploited for mill owners' gain. The young workers toiled under poor conditions for long hours only to return to dormitories that offered strict dress codes, lousy meals, and were ruled by matrons with an iron fist.

In response, the Lowell mill workers — some as young as eleven — did something revolutionary: the tight-knit group of girls and women organized a union. They marched and demonstrated against a 15 percent cut in their wages and for better conditions… including the institution of a ten-hour workday. They started newspapers. They proclaimed: "Union is power." They went on strike.

As the movement spread through other Massachusetts mill towns, some 500 workers united to form the Lowell Female Labor Reform Association (LFLRA) in 1844… the first organization of American working women to bargain collectively for better conditions and higher pay. Sarah Bagley was named the LFLRA's first president and she promptly led a petition-drive that forced the Massachusetts legislature to investigate conditions in the mills. Bagley not only fought to improve physical conditions, she argued that the female workers "lacked sufficient time to improve their minds," something she considered "essential for laborers in a republic."

As with many revolutionary notions, the LFLRA met much opposition in their efforts. Despite their inability to secure the specific changes they demanded, the Lowell Mill Girls laid a foundation for female involvement and leadership in the soon-to-explode American labor movement and they continue to inspire those who stand against injustice today. ⛓

TIMELINE:

1847: Women's rights activist Lucy Stone marries Henry Blackwell. At their wedding, they read a statement that read, in part: "We deem it a duty to declare that this act on our part implies no sanction of, nor promise of voluntary obedience to such present laws of marriage as refuse to recognize the wife as an independent, rational being."

1851: At a women's convention in Seneca Falls, former slave turned activist Sojourner Truth says: "That man over there says that woman needs to be helped into carriages and lifted over ditches… Nobody ever helps me into carriages, or over mud-puddles or gives me any best place. And ain't I a woman?"

07
ST. PATRICK'S BATTALION

During the buildup to the Mexican-American War (1846-8), scores of immigrant Irishmen joined the army for the $7 a month. "The U.S. anti-immigrant press of the time caricatured the Irish with simian features, portraying them as unintelligent and drunk and charging that they were seditiously loyal to the pope," Anne-Marie O'Connor wrote in the *Los Angeles Times* in 1997. "But cheap Irish labor was welcome. Irish maids became as familiar as Latin American nannies are today."

Harsh treatment did not end after the Irishmen enlisted in the armed forces. "Anglo soldiers often harassed them, beat them up," said Robert Ryal Miller, author of *Shamrock and Sword*.

President James Polk incited hostilities by sending U.S. troops into disputed territory… and many of those Irish soldiers who found themselves heading west to fight a war of conquest were Catholic.

"They resented the treatment of Catholic priests and nuns by the invading Protestants," explained Rodolfo Acuña, author of *Occupied America*.

"This is a story about assimilation," historian Peter F. Stevens added. "A lot of these guys deserted because of the anti-Catholic, anti-foreigner movement."

One such deserter was John Riley, an Irishman from Galway who swam across the Rio Grande after asking permission to go to Mass. "As the U.S. Army marched through Mexico's northern deserts, others followed, and Riley became captain of a 200-member rogue column in the Mexican army," explained O'Connor. "At San Luis Potosi, convent nuns presented them the hand-stitched banner that foreshadowed their eventual romanticization."

A wartime newspaper correspondent from New Orleans described the banner as made of "green silk, and on one side is a harp, surmounted by the Mexican coat of arms, with a scroll on which is painted, 'Libertad para la República Mexicana.' Underneath the harp is the motto 'Erin go Bragh' (Ireland for Ever). On the other side is a painting... made to represent St. Patrick, in his left hand a key and in his right a crook or staff resting upon a serpent."

The group was unofficially known as the "Irish Volunteers" but Mexicans often referred to the redheaded and ruddy-complexioned men as the "Red Guards." Formally, the unit was called the "San Patricio Company," a title that evolved into the more familiar "St. Patrick's Battalion." In five major battles, the San Patricios earned a reputation for bravery that peaked on August 20, 1847 at Churubusco where, over the course of three hours, 60 percent of the San Patricios were killed or captured by a numerically superior American army. One of the prisoners was Brevet Major John Riley.

"At their court-martial," O'Connor stated, "most San Patricios said they had been forced to desert by the Mexicans, or had too much to drink."

"They needed an excuse. They couldn't say 'I hated the United States,' so they said they weren't responsible," said Miller. In some cases — including Riley's — this defense was effective. While

50 San Patricios were sentenced to death, five others were pardoned and 15 others received a reduced sentence. Riley himself was given 50 lashes and was hot-iron branded with a two-inch letter "D" for deserter. The San Patricios who faced the gallows were hanged in their Mexican uniforms and buried in graves dug by Riley and the other branded prisoners.

The war was over and in the name of historical cleansing, the legend of St. Patrick's Battalion was essentially forgotten north of the border (except for the San Patricios column that marches in the San Francisco St. Patrick's Day parade each year). The same cannot be said for Mexico where there is even a San Patricios public school.

Former Mexican President Ernesto Zedillo called the desertions "an act of conscience" and said the men of St. Patrick's Battalion "listened to the voice of justice, dignity and honor, and joined Mexican patriots who faced an aggression that lacked any justification." ▯

TIMELINE:
1853: Dr. Elizabeth Blackwell, America's first female physician, opens a clinic at 207 East 7th St. in New York City.
1857: Frederick Douglass declares: "Those who profess to want freedom yet deprecate agitation are men who want crops without plowing up the ground; they want rain without thunder and lightning. They want the ocean without the roar of its many waters."
1857: Clarence Darrow, attorney for the damned, is born.

08
THOREAU LAYS THE FOUNDATION FOR KING AND GANDHI

Under a government which imprisons any
unjustly, the true place for a just man is in prison.

— **Henry David Thoreau (1817-1862)**

Mention the name Thoreau and you're bound to hear a reference to his 1854 book, *Walden*, and its role in the earliest days of environmental awareness. Like many of the folks in this book, however, the more radical aspects of his lifework have, in many cases, been erased from his standard bio. Nonetheless, Thoreau's work in the area of civil disobedience lives on in the efforts of Gandhi, King, and the many who joined these men in their struggles.

In 1849, Thoreau wrote *On the Duty of Civil Disobedience* in response to the war of conquest being waged by his country, the Mexican-American War. It was not his only form of anti-war protest. "The war had barely begun, the summer of 1846, when… Thoreau, who lived in Concord, Massachusetts, refused to pay his poll tax, denouncing the Mexican War," says Zinn. "He was put in jail and spent one night there."

Against Thoreau's wishes (and behind his back), his friends paid the tax and secured his freedom. Legend has it that when fellow writer Ralph Waldo Emerson visited Thoreau in jail, he asked: "Henry, what are you doing in there?" To which Thoreau is said to have replied: "Ralph, what are you doing out there?"

The essay that sprang from not only Thoreau's opposition to the war but his vocal stance against slavery has come to be known, simply, as *Civil Disobedience*... and is arguably the most influential work of the era.

"If... the machine of government... is of such a nature that it requires you to be the agent of injustice to another," Thoreau writes, "then, I say, break the law."

This basic but profound principle has inspired and influenced activists for generations. Mohandas K. Gandhi effectively utilized a version of civil disobedience in India's struggle for independence against the British. Dr. Martin Luther King, Jr. channeled both Thoreau and Gandhi in his leadership of a non-violent civil rights movement.

"I became convinced that non-cooperation with evil is as much a moral obligation as is cooperation with good," said King. "No other person has been more eloquent and passionate in getting this idea across than Henry David Thoreau. As a result of his writings and personal witness, we are the heirs of a legacy of creative protest." ⌼

TIMELINE:

1859 After leading a doomed but bloody slave rebellion, John Brown declares: "I am quite certain that the crimes of this guilty land will never be purged away but with blood."

1861 American Miners' Association (first national coal miners union) established.

January 1, 1863 Abraham Lincoln issues the Emancipation Proclamation.

July 1863 New York City Draft Riots.

09
UNCLE TOM'S CABIN MOVES AMERICA TOWARD ABOLITION

So you're the little woman that wrote the book that made this great war.
— **Abraham Lincoln to Harriet Beecher Stowe in 1862**

In 1850, the Fugitive Slave Law was passed and both Northerners and Southerners were now legally required to turn in runaway slaves. One year later, Harriet Beecher Stowe (1811-1896) wrote *Uncle Tom's Cabin* (or *Life Among the Lowly*) as a serial in an antislavery paper, *The National Era*. In 1852, the Boston publishing company Jewett published it as a book and, as they are wont to say, the rest is history.

Widely considered to be the first social protest novel published in the United States (and the first major novel to have a black hero), *Uncle Tom's Cabin* sold more copies — with the exception of *The Bible* — than any book had ever sold in America until that point with sales reaching 300,000 copies in the first year. As Kenneth C. Davis explains, *Uncle Tom's Cabin* may not be the great American novel, but "for a long time it was surely the most significant American novel."

Stowe's graphic depiction of slave life — based on true stories — personalized the issue, reclaiming it from the sanitized domain of courtroom legalese. Her story outraged some and inspired many others. To her critics, she answered with *A Key to Uncle Tom's Cabin* in 1853 to provide documentation that every incident in her book had actually happened.

While there is no doubt about the widespread influence of *Uncle Tom's Cabin*, there is one myth worth clearing up. "Stowe's fictional Uncle Tom was no Uncle Tom," says historian Richard Shenkman. "He was kindly, considerate, humane, and brave… In the plays based on her book… Tom is subservient and spineless. Only in the book is he noble."

"The copies can be counted, but the emotional impact can't be calculated so easily," says Davis. "It is safe to say that no other literary work since 1776, when Tom Paine's *Common Sense* incited a wave of pro-Independence fervor, has the political impact of *Uncle Tom's Cabin*." ♡

TIMELINE:

1863 The first black regiments fight for the North during the Civil War.

December 1865 The Thirteenth Amendment passes and slavery is abolished.

1865 Walt Whitman writes "O Captain! My Captain!"

10
LIZZIE JENNINGS GETS ON THE BUS

On July 16, 1854, Elizabeth "Lizzie" Jennings (1830-1901), a 24-year-old schoolteacher setting out to fulfill her duties as organist at the First Colored Congregational Church on Sixth Street and Second Avenue, fatefully waited for the bus on the corner of Pearl and Chatham. Getting around 1854 New York City often involved paying a fare to board a large horse-drawn carriage… the forerunner to today's behemoth motorized buses. For black New Yorkers like Jennings, it wasn't that simple.

Pre-Civil War Manhattan may have been home to the nation's largest African-American population and New York's black residents may have paid taxes and owned property, but riding the bus with whites, well, that was a different story. Some buses bore large "Colored Persons Allowed" signs, while all other buses — those without the sign — were governed by a rather arbitrary system of passenger choice.

"Drivers determined who could ride," journalist Jasmin K. Williams explains, adding that NYC bus drivers "carried whips to keep undesirable passengers off." This unfortunate arrangement was the focus of a burgeoning movement for public transportation equality with Rev. J.W.C. Pennington of the First Colored Congregational Church (where Jennings just so happened to play the organ) playing a major role.

Against such a volatile backdrop, Lizzie Jennings opted for a bus without the "Colored Persons Allowed" sign. The

New York Tribune described what happened next: "She got upon one of the Company's cars… on the Sabbath, to ride to church. The conductor undertook to get her off, first alleging the car was full; when that was shown to be false, he pretended the other passengers were displeased at her presence; but (when) she insisted on her rights, he took hold of her by force to expel her. She resisted."

The outraged Jennings told the conductor she was "a respectable person, born and raised in this city," calling him "a good-for-nothing, impudent fellow for insulting decent persons while on their way to church."

The *Tribune* picks up the story from there: "The conductor got her down on the platform, jammed her bonnet, soiled her dress and injured her person. Quite a crowd gathered, but she effactually resisted. Finally, after the car had gone on further, with the aid of a policeman they succeeded in removing her."

This would not be the end of it for, like Rosa Parks, Jennings' behavior was no impetuous act of resistance. "Jennings was well connected," says Williams. "Her father was an important businessman and community leader with ties to the two major black churches in the city." Not satisfied with the massive rally that took place the following day at her church, Elizabeth Jennings hired the law firm of Culver, Parker & Arthur and took the Third Avenue Railway Company to court.

In a classic "who knew?" situation, Jennings was represented by a 24-year-old lawyer named Chester A. Arthur… yes, he who would go on to become the 21st president upon the death of

James A. Garfield in 1881. The trial took place in the bus company's home base of Brooklyn — then a separate city — where, in early 1855, Judge William Rockwell of the Brooklyn Circuit Court ruled in the black schoolteacher's favor… in that 1855 sort of way: "Colored persons if sober, well behaved and free from disease, had the same rights as others and could neither be excluded by any rules of the Company, nor by force or violence," Rockwell declared.

Jennings claimed $500 worth of damages but as the *Tribune* put it, "Some jury members had peculiar notions as to colored people's rights," and she ended up with $225, plus another $22.50 for court costs. Regardless, just one day after the verdict, the Third Avenue Railway Company issued an order to admit African-Americans onto their buses.

By 1860, all of the city's street and rail cars were desegregated. ⌁

TIMELINE:
1866 Civil Rights Act of 1866 declares blacks to be citizens and denies states the power to restrict their rights.
1869 Alice Hamilton, the founder of occupational medicine and the first woman professor at Harvard Medical School, is born.
1870 Victoria Woodhall, feminist, socialist and free love advocate, becomes first woman to run for president of the U.S.

11
COXEY'S ARMY MARCHES TO WASHINGTON

The movement has attracted the attention of the country as nothing else in the way of agitation has ever done, and as nothing else without violence ever could have done.

— **Jacob S. Coxey, quoted in the *Washington Post*, April 21, 1894**

Mention the word "depression" and typically, you'll evoke images of 1930s bread lines and families escaping the Dust Bowl. However, during the nineteenth century, American workers endured many depressions. In the 1870s, for example, things got so bad that 90,000 workers had to sleep in police stations throughout New York City. Another economic crisis hit in 1893 and that one lasted for half a decade. Four million workers lost their jobs and almost one in five workers was jobless. Out of this dire situation grew Coxey's Army.

Jacob Sechler Coxey (1854-1951), a populist leader in Massillon, Ohio, proposed that Congress increase the amount of legal tender in circulation (Coxey went as far as naming his son "Legal Tender"). Then, pre-dating FDR's New Deal by 40 years, Coxey wanted that currency spent on public works… in the name of creating jobs for the unemployed.

To help bring this plan to fruition, Coxey, along with Carl Browne of California, hatched the idea of a "living petition." An army of unemployed men would descend upon the nation's capital and shed light on the problems of the working class.

Dubbing their army the "Commonweal of Christ," Coxey, Browne and some 100 men left Massillon on Easter Sunday, March 25, 1894 (among the marchers was a young Jack London). According to reports, the numbers reached as high as 20,000 but only 500-600 made it to Washington, D.C. On April 30 the U.S. soldiers met them… having been called out by President Grover Cleveland. The authorities fully understood the impact such a public display could have. "There is a colored population numbering 85,000 in this city, fully half of whom are unemployed and many of whom are vicious," explained W.G. Moore, chief of the D.C. Police. "We could not, of course, afford to permit any demonstration which would arouse them. Hence the thoroughness of our preparations."

Before Coxey could deliver his speech, he was arrested for walking on the grass and his army quickly disbanded.

Coxey's efforts did inspire other "industrial armies," especially on the Pacific Coast. In addition, some of his ideas found a home in New Deal programs and his bold march undoubtedly shaped the organization of future protests like the Bonus Army, Dr. King's March on Washington, the Million Man March, and more.

Carlos A. Schwantes, author of *Coxey's Army: An American Odyssey*, sums up: "The story of the Coxey movement is ultimately a case study of how ordinary citizens influence — or fail to influence — political and economic issues in modern America." ⛉

TIMELINE:

1872 P. B. S. Pinchback of Louisiana becomes America's first black governor. It would be 127 years before L. Douglas Wilder of Virginia became the second.

1875 Irish coal miners in Pennsylvania organize as the "Molly Maguires" (named for an Irish revolutionary organization).

1877 The last words of Crazy Horse: "We preferred our own way of living. We were no expense to the government. All we wanted was peace and to be left alone."

12
IDA M. TARBELL AND OTHER "MUCKRAKERS"

"There were writers of the early twentieth century who spoke for socialism or criticized the capitalist system harshly," says Howard Zinn, "not obscure pamphleteers, but among the most famous of American literary figures, whose books were read by millions."

One such writer was Ida M. Tarbell (1857-1944), part of the original "muckrakers" (a term — not exactly of endearment — coined by Teddy Roosevelt).

Born in Pennsylvania but frustrated in her journalistic efforts in America, Tarbell left for Paris to study at the Sorbonne. It was there that she began writing articles for American newspapers and magazines. Her popular and successful series on Napoleon for *McClure's* was quickly followed by another on Abraham Lincoln. Both were later published as books while Tarbell took full advantage of her notoriety to focus on the Standard Oil monopoly.

Motivated in part by Standard Oil causing her father to lose business when she was younger, Tarbell dug deep to uncover, among other dubious practices, a covert arrangement by which the oil giant received enormous price breaks from local railroads. Her sixteen-part series ran from 1901 until 1904 and was also published as a book. Fallout from the series and book directly resulted in a new antitrust precedent being handed down by the United States Supreme Court against the entire oil industry, along with Congress establishing a Department of Commerce and a Bureau of Corporations.

Other muckrakers from this time period included Lincoln Steffens, author of *Tweed Days in St. Louis*, a novel about municipal corruption; Jacob Riis, who exposed life in New York's slums in his book, *How the Other Half Lives*; and perhaps the most famous muckraker of all, Upton Sinclair.

"Sinclair's novel *The Jungle*, published in 1906, brought the conditions in the meatpacking plants of Chicago to the shocked attention of the whole country, and stimulated demand for laws regulating the meat industry," writes Zinn. "But also, through the story of an immigrant laborer, Jurgis Rudkus, it spoke of socialism, of how beautiful life might be if people cooperatively owned and worked and shared the riches of the earth. *The Jungle* was first published in the Socialist

...YOU'RE NOT SUPPOSED TO KNOW

newspaper *Appeal to Reason*; it was then read by millions as a book, and was translated into seventeen languages." ▭

TIMELINE:

1885 A.J. Muste, revolutionary pacifist, is born.

1886 Haymarket Square bombing brings anarchism to the national stage.

1886 Samuel Gompers organizes the American Federation of Labor (AFL) in New York City.

1890 National Woman Suffrage Association merges with the American Woman Suffrage Association to form the National American Woman Suffrage Association. Elizabeth Cady Stanton (1815-1902) is named as its first president.

13
EMMA GOLDMAN SPREADS ANARCHY IN THE U.S.A.

Considering it took Emma Goldman (1869–1940) nearly 1,000 pages to pen her autobiography when she still had a decade to live, it's obviously not possible to do justice to her life's work here. Instead, I'll offer enough of a sketch to hopefully provoke a more widespread examination and appreciation of not only Goldman's life and work, but the incredible and important history of the American anarchist community.

Whether she was speaking truth to power (and the powerless) within the dictatorship of the proletariat or the dictatorship of the dollar, Goldman always provoked a response. She dealt with issues like birth control, individual freedom, civil rights, feminism, sexual orientation, and fairness in the workplace long before many of these topics were either popular or fashionable. For her tireless and fearless efforts, she was censored, threatened, evicted, imprisoned, and eventually deported from the home of the brave.

"The history of the political activities of man proves that they have given him absolutely nothing that he could not have achieved in a more direct, less costly, and more lasting manner," Goldman declared about women's struggle for the vote. "As a matter of fact, every inch of ground he has gained has been through a constant fight, a ceaseless struggle for self-assertion, and not through suffrage. There is no reason whatever to assume any woman, in her climb to emancipation, has been, or will be, helped by the ballot."

Which brings us to, of course, her commitment to anarchism. While the term "anarchy" today usually invokes images of chaos and public disorder, to Goldman and her comrades, to be an anarchist was to espouse equality, freedom from coercive institutions, lack of a centralized government, and the end of capitalism. As hard as it might be to imagine in the age of video games, MTV, and cyberspace, Emma's lectures drew overflow crowds in every corner of America and even the corporate press reported on them the following day.

Goldman also shattered the establishment image of an anarchist as either a bomb-throwing lunatic or a four-eyed drone. Goldman embraced art, drama, music, nature, and life itself.

She worked as a nurse and a midwife, wrote and lectured on the theater, and forged passionate friendships and relationships that defied and transcended prison walls, oceans, language, and even social philosophy.

"My life — I had lived in its heights and its depths, in bitter sorrow and ecstatic joy, in black despair and fervent hope," she summed up in 1931. "I had drunk the cup to the last drop. I had lived my life." ☿

TIMELINE:

1892 Homestead strike (Steelworkers strike at Homestead, PA).

1894 American dance innovator Martha Graham is born.

1898 Scholar, athlete, performer, and activist Paul Robeson is born.

14
JACK JOHNSON WINS THE HEAVYWEIGHT CROWN

There was Muhammad Ali, of course. Before that, there was Joe Louis and Sugar Ray and Henry Armstrong explaining how you can't discriminate against a left hook. "But in 1908," says Ron Flatter of ESPN.com, "39 years before Jackie Robinson broke the color barrier in major league baseball, there was Jack Johnson (1878-1946) — the first black man to hold the world heavyweight championship."

Winning the title was the easy part for Johnson, easily the greatest boxer of his era and one of the most powerful counter-punchers ever to put on a pair of gloves. The hard part was getting white champions to fight him. The great Jim Jeffries retired without even giving Johnson a chance. This merely fueled Johnson's mission as he demolished all comers — white and black — and cultivated a high-profile public image. Sooner or later, there would be no one else left to fight.

"It wouldn't be until Dec. 26, 1908, that Johnson would finally get his shot at the title. He got it for the simplest of reasons," explains Flatter. "Champion Tommy Burns was guaranteed $30,000 to fight him."

Burns was no match for the much-larger Johnson and referee Hugh McIntosh stepped in to stop the bout in the 14th round before the world could witness a black man sending a white champion to the canvas.

Johnson was an outspoken champion… unafraid to make his mark in an openly racist society. "He had his own jazz band, owned a Chicago nightclub, acted on stage, drove flashy yellow sports cars, reputedly walked his pet leopard while sipping champagne, flaunted gold teeth that went with his gold-handled walking stick and boasted of his conquests of whites — both in and out of the ring," says Flatter.

The new champion's public image along with his defiant nature lured Jeffries out of retirement. The beloved former champion said, "I am going into this fight for the sole purpose of proving that a white man is better than a Negro." More than 22,000 fans came to Reno, Nevada on July 4, 1910 to watch the first "Fight of the Century."

"Johnson was faster, stronger and smarter than Jeffries, knocking him out with ease," says sportswriter Dave Zirin. After the fight, Jeffries admitted, "I could never have whipped Johnson at my best. I couldn't have hit him. No, I couldn't have reached him in 1,000 years."

Jeffries' honesty aside, the image of a white hero being humiliated by a superior black athlete was more than 1910 America could handle. "After Johnson's victory, there were race riots around the country — in Illinois, Missouri, New York, Ohio, Pennsylvania, Colorado, Texas and Washington, D.C.," says Zirin. "Most of the riots consisted of white lynch mobs attempting to enter black neighborhoods, and blacks fighting back."

Racist America fought back, too. If Johnson could not be defeated in the ring, the powers-that-be had to devise another method. Judge Kenesaw Mountain Landis (see chapter 24 on Lester Rodney), the future commissioner of baseball, charged Johnson with taking his white girlfriend, Lucy Cameron, across state lines for "immoral purposes," a violation of the Mann white slavery act.

Johnson was convicted, jumped bail, and spent seven years in exile. An obviously out-of-shape, 37-year-old Johnson returned to the ring and the public spotlight in Havana, Cuba, on April 5, 1915 to fight the giant challenger Jess Willard. Johnson dominated the fight until the 20th round but, unless stories of him throwing the fight are to be believed, he soon faded and was knocked out in the 26th round (at the time there was no limit on the number of rounds).

Johnson eventually surrendered to federal authorities in 1920 and remained in prison until July 9, 1921. According to the *Ring Record Book*, Johnson retired with a record of 79-8 with 46 knockouts, 12 draws and 14 no-decisions. He was a charter member of the Boxing Hall of Fame. His athletic exploits, however, cannot fully reflect Jack Johnson's impact on sport, culture, and society.

Zirin sums up: "Today when 'Driving While Black' is a daily reality for millions, and blacks suffer mass incarceration, learning about Johnson and his era can inspire us toward the kind of defiance we must bring to our own era." ▢

TIMELINE:
1900 Mark Twain, commenting on the Spanish-American War, says: "I have seen that we do not intend to free but to subjugate the Philippines. And so I am an anti-imperialist. I am opposed to having the eagle put its talons on any other land… I have a strong aversion to sending our bright boys out there to fight with a disgraced musket under a polluted flag."
1901 Louis Armstrong is born. He would go on to revolutionize American jazz. Dizzy Gillespie later said, "Armstrong's station in the history of jazz is umimpeachable. If it weren't for him, there wouldn't be any of us."
1903 W.E.B. DuBois writes *The Souls of Black Folk*.

15
HELEN KELLER OPPOSES U.S. INVOLVEMENT IN WORLD WAR I

In a textbook example of whitewashing, if today's America knows Helen Keller (1880-1968) at all, it's the easy-to-digest image portrayed in the 1962 film, *The Miracle Worker*. Brave, deaf, and blind girl "overcomes" all obstacles to inspire everyone she meets. "The Helen Keller with whom most people are familiar is a stereotypical sexless paragon who was able to overcome deaf-blindness and work tirelessly to promote charities and organizations associated with other blind and deaf-blind individuals," writes Sally Rosenthal in *Ragged Edge*.

But, in 1909, Helen Keller became a socialist. Soon after, she became a vocal supporter of the working class and traveled the nation to voice her opposition to war. "How can our rulers claim they are fighting to make the world safe for democracy," she asked, "while here in the U.S. Negroes may be massacred and their property burned?" Of course, as a woman with disabilities, she was patronized by the same mainstream media that previously championed her as a heroine. The editors of the *Brooklyn Eagle* wrote: "Her mistakes spring out of the manifest limitations of her development."

Keller minced no words in her response… one of which appeared in newspapers across America: "So long as I confine my activities to social services and the blind, the newspapers compliment me extravagantly, calling me an 'arch-priest of the sightless' and 'wonder woman.' But when I discuss poverty and the industrial system under which we live that is a different matter."

As the militaristic frenzy spread across America, Keller appeared at New York City's Carnegie Hall on January 5, 1916. "I have a word to say to my good friends, the editors, and others who are moved to pity me," she said. "Some people are grieved because they imagine I am in the hands of unscrupulous persons who lead me astray and persuade me to espouse unpopular causes and make me the mouthpiece of their propaganda. Now, let it be understood once and for all that I do not want their pity; I would not change places with one of them. I know what I am talking about. My sources of information are as good and reliable as anybody else's. I have papers and magazines from England, France, Germany and Austria that I can read myself. Not all the editors I have met can do that. Quite a number of them have to take their French and German second hand. No, I will not disparage the editors. They are an overworked, misunderstood class. Let them remember, though, that if I cannot see the fire at the end of their cigarettes, neither can they thread a needle in the dark. All I ask, gentlemen, is a fair field and no favor. I have entered the fight against preparedness and against the economic system under which we live. It is to be a fight to the finish, and I ask no quarter."

Keller's critique of the government propaganda campaign to stir up Americans to support U.S. intervention in the war remains more germane than ever. "Every modern war has had its root in exploitation," Keller said. "The Civil War was fought to decide whether the slaveholders of the South or the capitalists of the North should exploit the West. The Spanish-American War decided that the United States should exploit Cuba and the Philippines. The South African War decided that the British should exploit the diamond mines. The Russo-Japanese War decided that Japan should exploit Korea. The present war is to decide who shall exploit the Balkans, Turkey, Persia, Egypt, India, China, Africa. And we are whetting our sword to scare the victors into sharing the spoils with us. Now, the workers are not interested in the spoils; they will not get any of them anyway."

She urged workers — the ones who do the fighting and dying — to strike at the heart of America's drive toward war. "Strike against war, for without you no battles can be fought," she declared. "Strike against preparedness that means death and misery to millions of human beings. Be not dumb, obedient slaves in an army of destruction. Be heroes in an army of construction." ☿

TIMELINE:
1905 The Industrial Workers of the World (IWW) a.k.a. the Wobblies, hold their first meeting. In attendance are Eugene Debs, Mother Jones, and Big Bill Haywood.
1906 The Pure Food and Drug Act passes.
1908 Jack London writes *The Iron Heel*.
1912 Elizabeth Gurley Flynn leads Bread & Roses textile strike of 20,000 women, Lawrence, MA.

Patriot Words...
You're not to be so blind with patriotism that you can't face reality. Wrong is wrong, no matter who does it or says it.
— **Malcolm X**

16
EUGENE DEBS RUNS FOR PRESIDENT FROM A PRISON CELL

Eugene V. Debs (1855–1926) was one of the most prominent labor organizers and political activists of his time. He was also nominated as the Socialist Party's candidate for president five times. His voting tallies over his first four campaigns effectively illustrate the remarkable growth of the party during that volatile time period:

1900:   94,768
1904: 402,400
1908: 402,820
1912: 897,011

America's entrance into World War I, however, provoked a tightening of civil liberties, culminating with the passage of the Espionage and Sedition Act in June 1917. This totalitarian salvo read in part: "Whoever, when the United States is at war, shall willfully cause or attempt to cause insubordination, disloyalty, mutiny, or refusal of duty in the military or naval forces of the United States, shall be punished by a fine of not more than $10,000 or imprisonment of not more than 20 years, or both."

One year after the Espionage and Sedition Act was voted into law, Debs was in Canton, Ohio for a Socialist Party convention. He was arrested for making a speech deemed "anti-war" by the Canton district attorney. In that speech, Debs declared, "They have always taught and trained you to believe it to be your patriotic duty to go to war and to have yourselves slaughtered at their command. But in all the history of the world you, the people, have never had a voice in declaring war, and strange as it certainly appears, no war by any nation in any age has ever been declared by the people.

"Do not worry over the charge of treason to your masters, but be concerned about the treason that involves yourselves," he concluded. "Be true to yourself and you cannot be a traitor to any good cause on earth."

These words led to a 10-year prison sentence and the stripping of his U.S. citizenship. At his sentencing, Debs famously told the judge:

Your honor, years ago, I recognized my kinship with all living beings, and I made up my mind that I was not one bit better than the meanest on earth. I said then, and I say now, that while there is a lower class, I am in it; while there is a criminal element, I am of it; while there is a soul in prison, I am not free.

While serving his sentence in the federal penitentiary, Debs was nominated for the fifth time, campaigned from his jail cell, and remarkably garnered 917,799 votes. (In 2004, Leonard Peltier collected 25,101 votes while running for president from his prison cell.)

President Woodrow Wilson ignored all pleas to release Debs from prison. But, after serving 2 years and 8 months behind bars, President Warren G. Harding commuted his sentence on Christmas Day 1921.

The Espionage and Sedition Act is still on the books today. ⏳

TIMELINE:

1915 Anarchist Lucy Parsons leads hunger march in Chicago. IWW songwriter Ralph Chaplin writes "Solidarity Forever" for the march.

1916 Fannie Lou Hamer is born. She becomes a tireless crusader for black voting rights and leader of the Mississippi Freedom Democratic Party.

1919 Emma Goldman is sentenced to two years in a Missouri jail (and fined $10,000) for "conspiracy against draft." Alexander Berkman is sent to the Atlanta Penitentiary.

17
KATHERINE HEPBURN WEARS PANTS

Stockings are an invention of the devil.

— **Katherine Hepburn (1907-2003)**

It's the hallmark of innovation and rebellion that what once was outrageous is eventually mundane. After all, what could be more unremarkable than seeing a woman wearing a pair of pants?

When Katherine Hepburn shunned the girdles, petticoats, stockings, garter belts, and high heels considered "normal" for women of her time, she was brazenly defying fashion and social convention. Hepburn wore pants. She even wore sneakers. In 1930s Hollywood, such behavior was deemed scandalous… to say the least.

Reviews for the 1936 film *Sylvia Scarlett* — in which Hepburn spends almost its entirety in short hair and men's clothing — were sarcastic, to say the least. *Time* magazine declared "Hepburn is better-looking as a boy than a woman," while the *New York Herald-Tribune* named her "the handsomest boy of the season."

Her bosses at RKO went as far as commandeering Hepburn's slacks in the hope of forcing her to wear a skirt. Unmoved, Kate strolled the studio lot in only her underwear. Her point was made… and her pants were returned.

"If you obey all the rules, you miss all the fun," said Hepburn, and by doing what came naturally her public mutiny became a high-profile example of independence and individuality. ▯

TIMELINE:

August 26, 1920 Nineteenth Amendment is added to the Constitution, stating that the right of U.S. citizens to vote "shall not be denied… on account of sex."

1920 American Civil Liberties Union (ACLU) founded.

1921 Margaret Sanger founds the American Birth Control League in N.Y.C.

1921 The trial of Italian anarchists Nicola Sacco and Bartolomeo Vanzetti in Boston (after a long international struggle, they would be executed in 1927).

1924 The Society for Human Rights in Chicago, America's earliest known gay rights organization, is founded.

1920s Dorothy Parker out-talks and out-thinks the boys at the Algonquin Roundtable.

18
THE BONUS ARMY DEMANDS JUSTICE

In 1924, American soldiers who fought on the battlefields of World War I were voted "Adjusted Compensation" by Congress: $1.25 for each day served overseas, $1.00 for each day served in the States. To the "doughboys," the money was seen as a bonus… but it came with a catch. Their bonus was not payable until 1945.

In the spring and summer of 1932, disgruntled veterans — left broke and unemployed by the Depression — got the idea to demand payment on the future worth of the aforementioned certificates. Anywhere from 17,000 to 25,000 former doughboys formed a Bonus Expeditionary Force (BEF), otherwise known as the "Bonus Army," and — bonus certificates in hand — they marched on Washington to picket Congress and President Herbert Hoover.

While they may have fought in Europe as a segregated army, the men of the BEF did not invite Jim Crow to this battle. Arriving from all over the country, alone or with wives and children, they huddled together, mostly across the Potomac River from the Capitol, in what were called "Hoovervilles," in honor of the president who adamantly refused to hear their pleas.

The House of Representatives passed the Patman Bill for veterans' relief on June 15, 1932, but the bill met defeat in the Senate just two days later. More vets swarmed into the nation's capital. Shacks, tents, and lean-tos continued to spring up everywhere, and the government and newspapers decided to play the communist trump card for the umpteenth time. Despite the fact that the BEF was made up of 95 percent veterans, the entire group were labeled "Red agitators" — tantamount to declaring open season on an oppressed group of U.S. citizens. Right on cue, Hoover called out the troops… led by three soon-to-be textbook heroes.

The commander of the operation was Army Chief of Staff Douglas MacArthur, who branded the BEF as traitors bent on overthrowing the government, declaring, "pacifism and its bedfellow communism are all around us." MacArthur's young aide was none other than Dwight D. Eisenhower, while George S. Patton led the Third Cavalry — which spearheaded the eventual eviction of the Bonus Army. Patton shared MacArthur's hatred of "reds" and lectured his troops on how to deal with the BEF: "If you must fire do a good job — a few casualties become martyrs, a large number an object lesson… When a mob starts to move keep it on the run… Use a bayonet to encourage its retreat. If they are running, a few good wounds in the buttocks will encourage them. If they resist, they must be killed."

The three military icons got their chance on July 28, 1932 when a scuffle between the BEF and D.C. police resulted in two fatally wounded veterans. The U.S. Army assault integrated four troops of cavalry, four companies of infantry, a machine gun squadron, and six tanks. When asked by BEF leader Walter Waters if the Hooverville campers would be "given the opportunity to form in columns, salvage their belongings, and retreat in an orderly fashion," MacArthur replied: "Yes, my friend, of course." But, after marching up Pennsylvania Avenue, MacArthur's soldiers lobbed tear gas and brandished bayonets as they set fire to some of the tents. In a flash, the whole BEF encampment was ablaze.

"Disregarding orders — a common thread running through his career — MacArthur decided to finish the job by destroying the Bonus Army entirely," Kenneth C. Davis writes. "After nightfall, the tanks and cavalry leveled the jumbled camps of tents and packing-crate shacks. It was put to the torch."

Two veterans lost their lives in the assault and an eleven-week-old baby died from what was believed to be gas-related illness. In addition, an eight-year-old boy was partially blinded by gas, two policemen had their skulls fractured, and a thousand veterans suffered gas-related injuries.

After this impressive military success, the members of the Bonus Army were forced to leave Washington and many of them joined the other two million or so Americans who lived their lives on the road during the Great Depression.

"Some states, like California," Davis notes, "posted guards to turn back the poor."

Less than ten years later, MacArthur, Patton, and Eisenhower would be earning a place in history books by sending many of those same disenfranchised poor to grisly deaths on the battlefields of Europe and the Pacific. Meanwhile, the spirit of the Bonus Army lives on not only in the G.I. Bill of 1944 but in every sit-down strike, every march, and every demonstration for economic justice.

As the Washington *Evening Star* wrote during the Bonus Army's stay in D.C., "These men wrote a new chapter on patriotism of which their countrymen could be proud." ☿

TIMELINE:

1931 Nine black youths are put on trial for rape in Scottsboro, Alabama. The racist handling of the case results in a national outcry and Supreme Court intervention.

March 5, 1933 Franklin Delano Roosevelt is sworn in as president thus beginning the first "One Hundred Days" of the New Deal.

1934 Henry Miller writes *Tropic of Cancer*.

1935 Sinclair Lewis writes *It Can't Happen Here*.

19
BILLIE HOLIDAY SINGS "STRANGE FRUIT"

"Not many singers could claim to have 'suffered for their art' as Billie Holiday," says journalist Don Atapattu. "Born Elinore Harris… Billie certainly knew torment. As well as growing up black in the Jim Crow South; she endured sexual abuse; extreme poverty; homelessness; and a stint as a prostitute before she began recording music at the age of 18. Later in life she would survive chronic alcohol abuse, heroin addiction and regular beatings from the violent boyfriends her masochistic streak subconsciously picked."

Southern trees bear strange fruit,
Blood on the leaves and blood at the root

Billie Holiday (1915-1959) did not write "Strange Fruit."

Black bodies swinging in the southern breeze,
Strange fruit hanging from the poplar trees.

A former slave in America's post-Civil War South did not write it.

Pastoral scene of the gallant south,
The bulging eyes and the twisted mouth

"Strange Fruit" began as a poem… written in the 1930s by a Jewish schoolteacher from the Bronx.

After viewing a photograph of a lynching, Abel Meeropol was moved to pen the words Holiday would later make her own. Under the pseudonym "Lewis Allan," Meeropol set the poem to music and saw it first performed at a teachers' union meeting. It just as easily could have vanished in obscurity after that… but fate intervened.

Scent of magnolias, sweet and fresh,
Then the sudden smell of burning flesh.

When Barney Josephson, the manager of Cafe Society, a popular, desegregated Greenwich Village nightclub, heard "Strange Fruit," he arranged a meeting between Billie Holiday and Meeropol. After some initial hesitation, Lady Day wanted to record the song but her record label refused. Her persistence landed the song on a specialty label and Holiday began performing it regularly in live shows in 1939.

Here is fruit for the crows to pluck,
For the rain to gather, for the wind to suck,

Holiday's passionate interpretation of "Strange Fruit" introduced white audiences to powerful images of racism, inequality, and hate crimes… images that were now impossible to ignore. "'Strange Fruit' probably did more to put Billie on the map than anything she ever did," wrote Michael Brooks in the booklet that accompanied the three-CD box: *Billie Holiday – The Legacy*. "It was totally unlike any song written up to then, and it enraged those people it didn't scare."

For the sun to rot, for the trees to drop,
Here is a strange and bitter crop.

According to the Center for Constitutional Rights, between 1882 and 1968, mobs lynched 4,743 persons in the United States, over 70 percent of them African-American. ⌂

(Author's note: Abel Meeropol and his wife Anne later adopted Robert and Michael Rosenberg, the orphaned children of the executed Julius and Ethel Rosenberg.)

TIMELINE:

1936 Negro Leagues legend Josh Gibson (allegedly) becomes the only man to hit a ball clear out of Yankee Stadium.

1937 Americans volunteer to fight against the forces of fascism in the Spanish Civil War and become known as the Abraham Lincoln Brigade.

1938 Writing about the Louis-Schmeling heavyweight title fight, Richard Wright calls it "a colorful puppet show, one of the greatest dramas of make-believe ever witnessed in America."

20
THE FORGOTTEN VERSES OF "THIS LAND IS YOUR LAND"

If you were to open your mouth and belt out the words "this land is your land," you could rest assured that someone nearby would add: "this land is my land." The chorus to Woody Guthrie's 1940 classic is common knowledge… as are the first couple of verses.

But it isn't until you get to the later verses — the verses often omitted from official versions — that you start comprehendin' what good ol' Woody (1912-1967) had in mind:

As I was walkin' I saw a sign there
And that sign said "No tresspassin'"
But on the other side, it didn't say nothin'

Now that side was made for you and me
In the squares of the city/In the shadow of the steeple
Near the relief office, I see my people
And some are grumblin' and some are wonderin'
If this land's still made for you and me

Let's not forget that Guthrie penned the song in response to Irving Berlin's saccharine "God Bless America." Let's also not forget the words he scrawled on his guitar:

"This machine kills fascists."

Woody said: "This song is Copyrighted in U.S., under Seal of Copyright # 154085, for a period of 28 years, and anybody caught singin it without our permission, will be mighty good friends of ourn, 'cause we don't give a dern. Publish it. Write it. Sing it. Swing to it. Yodel it. We wrote it, that's all we wanted to do."

Guthrie laid the foundation for generations of American singer-songwriters to use their lyrics to challenge the saccharine platitudes of pop music. From Bob Dylan in the 1960s to Ani DiFranco today, American folk singers have provided a Greek chorus of protest and outrage to keep us all more honest and aware. ♫

TIMELINE:

April 9, 1939 Marian Anderson sings on the steps of the Lincoln Memorial.

1939 John Steinbeck writes *The Grapes of Wrath*.

21
DOROTHEA LANGE PHOTOGRAPHS
JAPANESE-AMERICAN INTERNMENT CAMPS

To live a visual life is an enormous undertaking, practically unattainable…
But I have only touched it, just touched it.

— Dorothea Lange (1895-1965)

More than just a "good war," former NBC newsman and *The Greatest Generation* author Tom Brokaw deemed WWII "the greatest war the world has seen." But what corporate media shills like Brokaw tend to omit is that the U.S. fought that war against racism with a segregated army. It fought the war to end atrocities by participating in the shooting of surrendering soldiers, the starvation of POWs, the deliberate bombing of civilians, wiping out hospitals, strafing lifeboats, and in the Pacific boiling flesh off enemy skulls to make table ornaments for sweethearts. And Franklin Delano Roosevelt, the leader of this anti-racist, anti-atrocity force, signed Executive Order 9066 in February 1942, interning over 100,000 Japanese-Americans without due process. Thus, in the name of taking on the architects of German prison camps he became the architect of American prison camps.

Through her work with farm families and migrant workers during the Great Depression, photographer Dorothea Lange was familiar with images of displacement. But, when she was hired by the War Relocation Authority to document life in Japanese neighborhoods, processing centers, and camp facilities, the racial and civil rights issues added a new dimension. "What was horrifying was to do this thing completely on the basis of what blood may be coursing through a person's veins, nothing else. Nothing to do with your affiliations or friendships or associations. Just blood," Lange said. As the Library of Congress wrote, "Lange quickly found herself at odds with her employer and her subjects' persecutors, the United States government."

"Lange's attempts to use her camera to expose the social impact of the mass incarcerations came into conflict with the authorities," says journalist Richard Phillips. "She was regarded with suspicion by the military, and even called before the War Relocation Authority on two occasions for alleged misuse of her photographs. The Wartime Civil Control Agency impounded most of her internment photographs, refusing to release them until after the war."

True to her belief that the camera could teach people "how to see without a camera," Lange created images of human dignity and courage in the face of vast injustice. But it wouldn't be until seven years after her death that her work would reach a wide audience. The Whitney Museum incorporated twenty-seven of Lange's Japanese internment camp images into an exhibit called "Executive Order 9066." *New York Times* critic A.D. Coleman subsequently called Lange's photographs "documents of such a high order that they convey the feelings of the victims as well as the facts of the crime." ⌨

TIMELINE:

1940 Richard Wright writes *Native Son*.

1941 Henry Miller writes *Air-Conditioned Nightmare*.

22
CHARLIE PARKER FINDS
THE PRETTY NOTES

*I'd been getting bored with the stereotyped changes (harmonies)
that were being used all the time. ... I found that by using the
higher intervals of a chord as a melody line and backing them
with appropriately related changes I could play the thing I'd
been hearing. I came alive.*

— Charlie Parker

The Kansas city-born Charlie "Bird" Parker (1920-1955) ushered
in a music revolution in mid-1940s New York City. Labeled "bebop,"
Bird's style built on earlier innovations by players like Coleman
Hawkins and Lester Young. Armed with revolutionary musical
vocabulary and style, Parker teamed with jazz legends like Dizzy
Gillespie, Bud Powell, Thelonious Monk, Charlie Christian,
Kenny Clarke, and Miles Davis… making Harlem the jazz capital
of the world and changing music forever.

One could describe Parker's sound as fast… for certain. One could explain that bebop introduced rhythmically asymmetrical improvisations and a new tonal vocabulary. One could also talk, as online encyclopedias do, about the use of "9ths, 11ths and 13ths of chords" or "rapidly implied passing chords" or perhaps "new variants of altered chords and chord substitutions."

For the intuitive Bird, however, it was "just music." He said all he was doing was "playing clean and looking for the pretty notes."

"First and foremost, he was a brilliant musician who revolutionized jazz," wrote Marilyn Marshall in *Ebony* Magazine. "A master of improvisation, Parker played the alto sax as it had never been played before. Jay McShann, the Kansas City bandleader and pianist who hired Parker for his group in 1938, says Parker was so good that, 'He not only influenced saxophone players, but influenced trumpet players, bass players, piano players — everybody.'"

"Bird's mind and fingers work with incredible speed," jazz critic Leonard Feather said when Parker burst onto the scene. "He can imply four chord changes in a melodic pattern where another musician would have trouble inserting two. His conception and execution bring to mind Tadd Dameron's comparison of the new jazz with the old: 'It's as if you had two roads, both going in the same direction, but one of them was straight with no scenery around it, and the other twisted and turned and had a lot of beautiful trees on all sides.' Charlie Parker takes you along that second road."

Again, leave it to a jazzman to explain things more simply. Legendary bassist Charles Mingus put it like this: "Bird sometimes could make the whole room feel as he did."

23
BRANDO'S UNDERSHIRT

When he stepped onto the stage in his white undershirt in 1947, Marlon Brando (1924-2004) revolutionized American acting. "He burst onto our consciousness wearing a torn T-shirt, mumbling, growling, scowling, screaming for 'Stel-la!' as Stanley Kowalski in Tennessee Williams' 'A Streetcar Named Desire,' first on Broadway, then on film," wrote Lawrence Grobel in his book *Conversations with Brando*. "From the beginning, Brando unleashed a raw power that had never been seen before on the screen."

In the role of Stanley Kowalski, Brando, says Andy Seiler of *USA Today*, "made theatrical history with his brutish yet complex performance."

It was no accident that Brando would commandeer the Kowalski role. He drove all the way to Provincetown to personally audition for Williams who, it's said, knew instantly that he had his lead. Brando would be the actor to lure audiences into empathizing with Stanley, making the character's actions later in the play that much more profound. Thus was the power of "The Method," the style of acting Brando came to represent… for better or for worse.

"He didn't invent 'method acting' (Stanislavsky did), but he made the term familiar around the world, revolutionizing the actor's art with his natural, tortured and spontaneous early performances," Seiler says.

As Jack Nicholson once said of Brando: "He gave us our freedom."

Speaking of freedom, Brando's reach far exceeded the stifling limits of stage and screen. He marched in support of fair housing, participated in anti-nuclear rallies, spoke out about the plight of Native Americans, and famously bowed out of the lead role of a film (*The Arrangement*) to devote himself to the civil rights movement.

"In the aftermath of the slaying of Dr. Martin Luther King, Jr. one of the most total commitments made to Dr. King's work by anyone came from Academy Award winning actor Marlon Brando," wrote Louie Robinson in the May 1968 issue of *Jet* magazine.

"If the vacuum formed by Dr. King's death isn't filled with concern and understanding and a measure of love," Brando declared on national television, "then I think we all are really going to be lost here in this country."

"He is considered by many to be… the man who changed the style of the movies, the most influential and widely imitated actor of his generation," concluded Grobel. "He is one of the select artists who will doubtless be remembered into the next century." ⌗

1942 Birth of Black Panther Party founder Huey P. Newton.

1940s A total of 6,770,000 workers take part in 14,000 strikes during WWII.

24
LESTER RODNEY HELPS BREAK BASEBALL'S COLOR LINE

In 1937, baseball was a segregated, primarily Eastern sport… but in the off-season, major leaguers often competed against Negro League teams in California. Against that backdrop, second-year phenom Joe DiMaggio was asked to name the toughest pitcher he had ever faced. Without hesitation, the Yankee Clipper told a group of reporters: "Satchel Paige."

Predictably, Joe D.'s honest appraisal went unmentioned in the next day's newspapers... with one exception. Lester Rodney (b. 1911) not only reported DiMaggio's comment, he made it a huge headline in the sports pages of the *Daily Worker*, the newspaper of the U.S. Communist Party.

The Brooklyn-born Rodney waged a relentless and effective campaign to publicly excoriate and humiliate baseball's commissioner, Judge Kenesaw Mountain Landis. "A blatant racist," Rodney called Landis. "The baseball owners of that period couldn't have picked a more appropriate man to represent their policies. He simply kept denying that there was a color barrier. I would write stories with headlines like 'Can You Read, Judge Landis?' and 'Can You Hear, Judge Landis?'

I know we got to him. The *Daily Worker* didn't have a big circulation, but we got noticed, and what we wrote was read by people in baseball and by other journalists."

Arnold Rampersad, Jackie Robinson's biographer, concurred: "In the campaign to end Jim Crow in baseball, the most vigorous efforts came from the Communist Press… notably from Lester Rodney."

Appropriately, Rodney was in the press box when Jackie Robinson played his first game with the Brooklyn Dodgers and remained there to witness both the abuse Robinson took and his eventual acceptance as a teammate.

When Robinson joined the Dodgers in 1947, outfielder Carl Furillo announced, "I ain't gonna play with no nigger." Fast-forward two years to an "important game in a close race" against the Braves. Rodney sets the scene: It's a scoreless tie in the top of the fifth with the Braves batting… Jim Russell on first, one out. Clint Conatser drives one in the right center gap. Furillo, owner of the best arm in baseball, catches up to the ball about 380 feet from home plate as Russell chugs around the bases.

"Freeze the action for a moment," Rodney suggests. "The long-legged Russell is in full cry, tearing through third in a wide turn. Conatser digs towards second. Robinson eases out some fifty feet into the outfield, half-facing Furillo. Shortstop (Pee Wee) Reese moves to cover second. First baseman Gil Hodges moves into position to possibly cut off the throw to the plate. Catcher Roy Campanella, the team's second black player, who came aboard in 1948, waits slightly up the third base line. (Pitcher Preacher) Roe ambles from the mound to back up the plate. It's the full panorama of baseball, a team game, in a moment that no television camera can encompass."

When we unfreeze, Furillo cuts loose with a throw "that bullets into Robinson's glove, head high, slightly to the right, making it unnecessary for him to pivot his feet before throwing." Robinson fires home to Campanella. Russell is out. The next batter pops up. The inning and the threat are history. Furillo jogs in from the outfield as Robinson, Roe, and Campanella wait for him at the lip of the dugout. The four men embrace. Rodney recalls leaning out of the press box "to watch them descend into the dugout together, then turn my gaze to the people in the stands, those raucous, salty, kidding, good-natured, integrated Ebbets Fields stands."

It took seven more years for the Brooklyn Dodgers to finally beat the hated Yankees in the World Series… but when they did, Furillo greeted Jackie and his wife Rachel at the celebratory party with an emotional cheek-to-cheek hug, crying, "We did it, we did it."

They did it, all right… with more than a little help from Lester Rodney. ⌻

TIMELINE:
1940s 350,000 cases of draft evasion during WWII.
1945 Bob Marley born.
1949 Paul Robeson says: "I happen to love America very much, not Wall Street and not your press."

25
JACKSON POLLOCK DRIPS HIS WAY ONTO THE COVER OF *LIFE* MAGAZINE

We have mechanical means of representing objects in nature, such as the camera and the photograph. The modern artist is expressing an inner world, expressing the energy, the motion, and other inner forces. The modern artist is working with space and time, and expressing his feelings rather than illustrating.

— Jackson Pollock (1912-1956)

When reporting on the infamous New York school of abstract expressionist painters in 1947, art critic Clement Greenberg pondered, "What can fifty do against one hundred and forty million?" It wasn't so much an entire population stacked *against* a band of radical painters that Greenberg was contemplating… rather it was 140 million Americans essentially *ignoring* a movement that would eventually change the face of art.

That all changed on August 8, 1949, when Jackson Pollock appeared on the cover of *Life* magazine. Suddenly, a new art vocabulary was born and Americans were imposing themselves onto the international art scene like never before. Pollock — and others like Mark Rothko, Willem de Kooning, and Robert Motherwell — had revolutionized the art world by shattering painterly pretensions and deconstructing the very concept of expression. What tied this group of "action painters" together was not a particular style but a spirit… the spirit of revolt. No one better exemplified this radical freedom of expression than the man *Time* magazine called Jack the Dripper.

Transplanted from Cody, Wyoming, Pollock worked for the Federal Art Project from 1938 to 1942. Shortly after that, he abandoned traditional painting techniques and trusted his instincts. This included laying massive canvases on the floor where he could circle and stalk… dripping and dribbling not just traditional paint but house paint, nails, coins, and the stray cigarette butt.

"On the floor I am more at ease," Pollock declared in 1947. "I feel nearer, more a part of the painting, since this way I can walk around in it, work from the four sides and be literally 'in' the painting."

De Kooning put it simply: "He broke the ice." Therein lies the rebellion. Pollock and his contemporaries painted what they felt with little concern for rules or conventions or critical understanding. When one critic wrote that Pollock's paintings lacked a beginning or an end, the painter replied, "He didn't mean it as a compliment, but it was."

Even as he became a cultural icon, Pollock's personal life was a never-ending melodrama of alcohol, brawls, and self-doubt. He died in a car accident in 1956… thus fulfilling his own prophecy: "The problem isn't painting; it's what to do when you aren't painting." ⌁

TIMELINE:
1951 The Mattachine Society, the first nationwide gay rights organization, is formed by Harry Hay.

Patriot Words…
Totalitarianism is patriotism institutionalized.
— **Steve Allen**

26
SALT OF THE EARTH IS FILMED

The continuing significance of Salt of the Earth *for our own time arises from its attempt — rare in works of art in any medium — to integrate the struggles of women, of an ethnic minority, and workers.*

— Deborah Rosenfelt, author of a book about the film

Name the best-known early 1950s film with a union theme. Easy. That would be *On the Waterfront*. But *Waterfront* was not the early 1950s film with a union theme that none other than Noam Chomsky called, "one of the greatest films ever made...couldn't get it out of my mind for weeks." That would be the sadly neglected *Salt of the Earth* (1953).

Made by a group of McCarthy-era, blacklisted filmmakers, *Salt of the Earth* tells the story of New Mexico zinc miners — and their families — struggling against their bosses for a better life. The film is based on the real-life struggle of MMSW Local 890, which went on strike against the Empire Zinc Corporation in 1950.

"Shortly after the strike had begun, an injunction prohibited men from walking the picket lines," writes Tony Pecinovsky in *People's Weekly World*. "Women soon replaced their brothers, sons, husbands and fathers – an action of major significance, especially since corporate America had little tolerance for people of color, especially women of color, standing up for their rights."

Narrated by a character appropriately named Esperanza, the wife of a striking miner, *Salt of the*

Earth featured a cast made up almost entirely of those who actually participated in the strike and was a feminist movie before such a thing had a name. Writing in *Cineaste*, Ruth McCormick states that no other film "deals as basically and as thoroughly… with the issue of women's liberation, from the politics of housework to the myth of male supremacy, the ways in which class society divides the sexes by creating false antagonism between them."

Equally as impressive is the manner in which the revolutionary film was completed against all odds. Production began on January 20, 1953 and the *Hollywood Reporter* soon announced: "H'wood Reds are shooting a feature-length anti-American racial issue propaganda movie." The outcry carried all the way to Congress where Donald Jackson, a member of the House Un-American Activities Committee (HUAC), promised: "I shall do everything in my power to prevent the showing of a communist-made film in the theaters of America." Rosaura Revueltas, the woman who played Esperanza, was deported to Mexico during production on a trumped-up immigration charge (her passport hadn't been stamped upon entering the U.S.).

"The film's director, Herbert Biberman, spent six months in jail for refusing to testify before HUAC," adds Pecinovsky. "Several key personnel on the film were found in contempt of Congress when they refused HUAC's badgering as well. The film crew was barred from laboratories, sound studios, and other facilities normally used by filmmakers. No Hollywood labs would process the film and the projectionist's union refused to show it."

Salt of the Earth made its theatrical debut in March 1954 and won the International Grand Prize from the Academie du Cinema de Paris in 1955. Like the characters in the film and the real-life workers those characters were based on, the filmmakers had emerged triumphant in what Pecinovsky calls a story "about racism, sexism, chauvinism, red-baiting, union busting, censorship and courage; the courage of ordinary people, workers and filmmakers, standing together in solidarity."

"The villain in *Salt of the Earth* is discrimination," adds film critic Danny Peary.

"*Salt of the Earth...* inspires belief in the possibility of genuine social change," Rosenfelt concludes. "It encourages us to act on that belief. Seeing it has made a difference in more than one life; my own was one of them." ▯

TIMELINE:

1952 Ralph Ellison writes *Invisible Man*.

1952 The Immigration and Naturalization Act passes, removing racial and ethnic barriers to naturalization.

May 17, 1954 In the unanimous opinion in *Brown v. Board of Education of Topeka*, Chief Justice Earl Warren writes: "We conclude that in the field of public education the doctrine of 'separate but equal' has no place."

1953 Julius and Ethel Rosenberg are sentenced to death for espionage.

1954 The Food and Drug Administration (FDA) files a Complaint for Injunction against Wilhelm Reich in the Federal Court in Portland, Maine. Two years later, the FDA supervises the burning of several tons of Reich's publications.

27
I. F. STONE GOES *WEEKLY*

Every government is run by liars and nothing they say should be believed.

— **I. F. Stone**

Born Isidor Feinstein, the incomparable I. F. Stone (1907–1989) served as an editor at the *Nation* and worked for several other papers before founding his own journal in 1953 with $3,000 borrowed from a friend and a 5,300-name subscription list inherited from a handful of defunct lefty publications. *I. F. Stone's Weekly* reached a circulation of 70,000 by the 1960s and Stone was widely praised — even by his enemies — for his investigative skills and his ability to see through the hype. Victor Navasky of the *Nation* wrote that "Izzy" was "right about McCarthyism, right about the war in Vietnam (he was one of the first to raise questions about the authenticity of the Gulf of Tonkin incident), right about the Democrats' repeated failure to live up to their own principles, right about what he called, long before the U.S. invasion of Iraq, the 'Pax Americana.'"

"I. F. Stone was the modern Tom Paine — as independent and incorruptible as they come," said Ralph Nader. "Notwithstanding poor eyesight and bad ears, he managed to see more and hear more than other journalists because he was curious and fresh with the capacity for both discovery and outrage every new day."

Without high-placed sources or invitations to the big press conferences, Stone scooped the big name reporters time and time again. He scoured public documents, studied the transcripts of Congressional committee hearings, and searched the large newspapers for inspiration. Stone once told David Halberstam that the *Washington Post* was an exciting paper to read, "because you never know on what page you would find a page-one story."

"What Stone never talked about was the effect he had on many reporters who, often without attribution, 'lunched off' his scoops," said Nader. "He taught them courage and insistence without ever meeting them… while others in his profession cowered, he stood tall to challenge the abusers of power no matter where they came from — right, middle or left."

In an attempt to explain why he risked his career and ventured out on his own to create the *Weekly*, Stone explained: "To give a little comfort to the oppressed, to write the truth exactly as I saw it, to make no compromises other than those of quality imposed by my own inadequacies, to be free to follow no master other than my own compulsions, to live up to my idealized image of what a true news-paperman should be, and still be able to make a living for my family — what more could a man ask?"

Postscript: Late in his life, I. F. Stone studied classical Greek and penned the surprise best seller, *The Trial of Socrates* in 1988. ⚥

TIMELINE:

1953 James Baldwin writes *Go Tell it On the Mountain*.

1955 Rosa Parks refuses to give up her seat on the bus.

1956 Allen Ginsberg writes "Howl."

1956 The Daughters of Bilitis, the first modern lesbian organization, is formed.

1957 Louis Armstrong says: "The way they are treating my people in the South, the government can go to hell."

28
LOLITA LEBRÓN AND OTHERS ATTACK CONGRESS

No other woman in the Hemisphere has been in prison on such charges for so long a period [as Lolita Lebrón]; a fact which Communist critics of your human rights policy are fond of pointing out.

— National Security Advisor, Zbigniew Brzezinski,
   in a secret memo to President Jimmy Carter in 1979

When early American revolutionaries chanted, "Give me liberty or give me death" and complained of having but one life to give for their country, they became the heroes of our history textbooks. But, thanks to the power of the U.S. media and education industries, the Puerto Rican nationalists who dedicated their lives to independence are known as criminals, fanatics, and assassins.

On March 1, 1954, in the gallery of the House of Representatives, Congressman Charles A. Halleck rose to discuss with his colleagues the issue of Puerto Rico. At that moment, Lolita Lebrón (b. 1919) alongside three fellow freedom fighters, having purchased a one-way train ticket from New York (they expected to be killed) unfurled a Puerto Rican flag and shouted "Free Puerto Rico!" before firing eight shots at the roof. Her three male co-conspirators aimed their machine guns at the legislators. Andrés Figueroa's gun jammed, but shots fired by Rafael Cancel Miranda and Irving Flores injured five congressmen.

"I know that the shots I fired neither killed nor wounded anyone," Lebrón stated afterwards, but with the attack being viewed through the sensationalizing prism of American tabloid journalism, this did not matter. She and her nationalist cohorts became prisoners of war for the next twenty-five years.

Why prisoners of war? To answer that, we must recall that since July 25, 1898, when the United States illegally invaded its tropical neighbor under the auspices of the Spanish-American War, the island has been maintained as a colony. In other words, the planet's oldest colony is being held by its oldest representative democracy — with U.S. citizenship imposed without the consent or approval of the indigenous population in 1917. It is from this geopolitical paradox that the Puerto Rican independence movement sprang forth.

This movement is based firmly on international law, which authorizes "anti-colonial combatants" the right to armed struggle to throw off the yoke of imperialism and gain independence. UN General Assembly Resolution 33/24 of December 1978 recognizes "the legitimacy of the struggle of peoples for independence, territorial integrity, national unity and liberation from colonial domination and foreign occupation by all means available, particularly armed struggle."

Prison did not dampen Lebrón's revolutionary spirit as she attended demonstrations and spoke out to help win the long battle to eject the U.S. Navy from the tiny Puerto Rican island of Vieques in 2003. ⌺

TIMELINE:
1957 Jack Kerouac writes *On the Road*.
1957 The Committee for a SANE Nuclear Policy is founded.
1957 Southern Christian Leadership Council (SCLC) is founded.
1959 John Cassavetes' *Shadows* is released.

29
RACHEL CARSON INSPIRES THE MODERN ENVIRONMENTAL MOVEMENT

Can anyone believe it is possible to lay down such a barrage of poison on the surface of the earth without making it unfit for all life? They should not be called "insecticides" but "biocides."
— Rachel Carson (1907–1964)

Sounding a toxic wake-up with the publication of her book *Silent Spring* in 1962, Rachel Carson simultaneously alerted a nearly comatose public to the chemical dangers all around them while incurring the predictable wrath of corporate America. Indeed, an author can be certain about his or her impact when companies like Monsanto — the good people who brought us Agent Orange and bovine growth hormone — take aim.

The use and abuse of pesticides, herbicides, and fungicides, Carson posited, were directly responsible for myriad health hazards not only for humans, but all life on the planet. While I would argue that Rachel Carson did not go far enough in her condemnation, there is little debate that *Silent Spring* was a much-needed call-to-arms for the budding environmental movement.

"If the Bill of Rights contains no guarantee that a citizen shall be secure against lethal poisons distributed either by private individuals or by public officials," she wrote, "it is surely because our forefathers… could conceive of no such problem."

Carson's alarming prognosis, however, was not lost on some of the legislators of her day. After appearing at Senate hearings in 1963, Senator Abraham Ribicoff of Connecticut became so moved by her testimony, he asked her to autograph his copy of *Silent Spring*. Clearly, her clarion call would not go completely ignored.

"*Silent Spring* showed that people are not master of nature, but rather part of nature," says Carson's biographer, John Henricksson. "It was a revolutionary thought at the time. Today no one seriously questions its truth, but in 1962 it was a direct attack on the values and assumptions of a society." ▯

TIMELINE:

1960 Pacifica Radio is created.

1960 Mort Sahl makes the cover of *Time* magazine, dubbed "the patriarch of a new school of comedians."

1961 James Baldwin identifies "the two most powerful movements" in America as the student integrationist movement and the Nation of Islam. Baldwin sides with the civil rights movement but admits "the Muslim movement has all the evidence on its side."

1961 Black Americans, organized by Maya Angelou and others, protest in front of the United Nations after the assassination of Patrice Lumumba in the Congo.

1962 Illinois becomes the first state to decriminalize homosexual acts between consenting adults in private.

1962 James Meredith becomes the first black student at the University of Mississippi.

30
BETTY FRIEDAN ASKS: "IS THAT ALL?"

The core of the problem today is not sexual but a problem of identity —
a stunting of growth that is perpetuated by the feminine mystique.
— Betty Friedan

When Betty Friedan (b. 1921) attended her fifteenth college reunion at Smith College, she conducted a survey among her fellow alumni. What the women she spoke to had to say about the state of their lives eventually became a book that, upon its release in 1963, would spark a national debate about a woman's role in American society. *The Feminine Mystique* begins, famously:

The problem lay buried, unspoken, for many years in the minds of American women. It was a strange stirring, a sense of dissatisfaction, a yearning that women suffered in the middle of the twentieth century in the United States. Each suburban wife struggled with it alone. As she made the beds, shopped for groceries, matched slipcover material, ate peanut butter sandwiches with her children, chauffeured Cub Scouts and Brownies, lay beside her husband at night — she was afraid to ask even of herself the silent question — "Is this all?"

"The book reached millions of readers," says Kenneth C. Davis. "Women were… suddenly discussing the fact that society's institutions — government, mass media and advertising, medicine and psychiatry, education, and organized religion — were systematically barring them from becoming anything more than housewives and mothers."

Far from a manifesto, *The Feminine Mystique* focused almost exclusively on white middle-class women and eschewed radical solutions. Nonetheless, the book was a crucial catalyst in the re-launching of the relatively dormant women's rights movement conceptualized by earlier feminists like Emma Goldman and Margaret Sanger. Friedan herself recognized her obligation to take things further.

"I realized that it was not enough just to write a book," says Friedan. "There had to be social change. And I remember somewhere in that period coming off an airplane [and] some guy was carrying a sign." That sign, which read, "The first step in revolution is consciousness," inspired Friedan to puts words into action by founding the National Organization for Women, the National Women's Caucus, and the National Abortion Rights Action League.

Viewed through the prism of the twenty-first century, Friedan's critique appears obvious… even tame. But that is the essence of social change. Initially rejected, new ideas are typically co-opted and eventually taken for granted. Friedan and her book played their role; it's the work of today's feminists that takes the struggle to the next level. ◻

TIMELINE:

1963 Timothy Leary is dismissed from Harvard.

1963 The Supreme Court rules that all criminal defendants must have legal counsel and all illegally acquired evidence is inadmissible in state and federal courts.

1963 Manning Marable says: "In three difficult years, the southern struggle had grown from a modest group of black students demonstrating peacefully at one lunch counter to the largest mass movement for racial reform and civil rights in the twentieth century."

1963 In his "Letter from a Birmingham Jail," Martin Luther King writes: "The Negro's greatest stumbling block in the stride toward freedom is… the white moderate who is more devoted to 'order' than to justice."

1963 W.E.B. DuBois, living in Ghana at the age of 95, renounces his U.S. citizenship.

31
RALPH NADER WRITES *UNSAFE AT ANY SPEED*

A great problem of contemporary life is how to control the power of economic interests which ignore the harmful effects of their applied science and technology.
— **Ralph Nader**

Ralph Nader (b. 1934) has been called "the most vigilant citizen in America," and Citizen Ralph's first high-profile salvo against the automobile industry was a 1959 article called "The Safe Car You Can't Buy," in the *Nation*. Nader wrote: "It is clear Detroit today is designing automobiles for style, cost, performance, and calculated obsolescence, but not — despite the 5,000,000 reported accidents, nearly 40,000 fatalities, 110,000 permanent disabilities, and 1,500,000 injuries yearly — for safety."

Six years later, in 1965, Nader published *Unsafe at Any Speed: The Designed-In Dangers of the American Automobile* and the consumer movement was born. The book meticulously detailed how car companies sacrificed safety in the name of profit. For example, General Motors' Chevrolet Corvair had a suspension that made it liable to roll over.

The response from GM made Nader a folk hero. Private detectives were hired to trap the consumer crusader in a compromising situation, but they failed. Nader caught wind of the plot and sued the auto giant for invasion of privacy. The fallout was swift and far-reaching. GM President James Roche was forced to appear before a nationally televised Senate subcommittee and apologize to Nader; GM improved the Corvair's suspension; and Congress passed the 1966 National Traffic and Motor Vehicle Safety Act.

Nader used the majority of his $284,000 settlement to lay the groundwork for a long-term consumer rights movement. Public Citizen, the NGO he founded in 1971, has been credited with helping to pass the Safe Drinking Water Act and Freedom of Information Act and prompting the creation of the Occupational Safety and Health Administration (OSHA), Environmental Protection Agency (EPA), and Consumer Product Safety Commission (CPSC), and spawned divisions such as Citizen Action Group, Congress Watch, Global Trade Watch, and Tax Reform Research Group. Non-profit organizations created by Nader include the Corporate Accountability Research Project, Disability

Rights Center, National Citizens' Coalition for Nursing Home Reform, and the National Coalition for Universities in the Public Interest.

"Nader's accomplishments have become part of the fabric of American public life," Karen Croft writes in Salon. "He works harder than any president or member of Congress," says Croft. "He has affected your life as a consumer more than any man, but you didn't elect him and you can't make him go away."

Croft asked Nader how he wants to be remembered, to which he replied: "For helping strengthen democracy, for making raw power accountable and enhancing justice and the fulfillment of human possibilities." ⌑

TIMELINE:

1964 Freedom Summer (a campaign in the Deep South to register blacks to vote).

1964 John Coltrane releases *A Love Supreme*.

1964 Dick Gregory writes *Nigger*.

1964 Martin Luther King, Jr. receives Nobel Peace Prize.

1964 Malcolm X arrives at Cassius Clay's training camp in Miami.

1964 Sam Cooke sings: "I go to the movies and I go downtown/somebody keeps telling me don't hang around/it's been a long time coming but I know/a change is gonna come, oh yes it will."

1964 After attending the Republican Convention that nominated Barry Goldwater for president, Jackie Robinson says: "I had a better understanding of how it must have felt to be a Jew in Hitler's Germany."

32
NAKED LUNCH IS DECLARED "NOT OBSCENE"

First published in 1959 by Maurice Girodias and Olympia Press, *Naked Lunch* quickly became infamous across Europe… even in countries where it was banned. This controversial, groundbreaking, and uniquely structured (or unstructured?) work by Beat legend William S. Burroughs (1914-1997), says *Poets & Writers*, "renders an urban wasteland of paranoid police, raving sex addicts, and psychotic doctors through the eyes of a narcotics junky."

How far was it ahead of its time? In 1964, counterculture icon Terry Southern called *Naked Lunch* "an absolutely devastating ridicule of all that is false, primitive, and vicious in current American life: the abuses of power, hero worship, aimless violence, materialistic obsession, intolerance, and every form of hypocrisy." Again: that was 1964.

Further proof of the novel's reach and impact lies in its prosecution as "obscene" by the state of Massachusetts in 1965 (soon followed by other states). Among those who served as an expert witness in defense of Burroughs and his vision was Norman Mailer (Massachusetts Superior Court Judge Eugene Hudson famously asked Mailer if any of his own novels involved "sex in the naked sense.")

"There is a kind of speech that is referred to as gutter talk that often has a very fine, incisive, dramatic line to it," Mailer testified, "and Burroughs captures that speech like no American writer I know." Commenting on the experimental style of *Naked Lunch*, Mailer pronounced, "I have no idea how the book was put together. The ingredients are so exceptional, like you have a banquet of thirty, forty components. You may eat in any order. You may shift them. The themes are so deeply entwined; any page put with another page creates an aura. It was so profoundly conceived."

The trial combined such testimony with facts such as the words "Fuck, shit, ass, cunt, prick, asshole, and cocksucker" appearing a combined total of 234 times on 235 pages… and eventually Hudson ruled against the book.

A year later, the Massachusetts Supreme Judicial Court declared the work "not obscene" thus upholding the U.S. Supreme Court's Brennan doctrine (the decision that cleared Henry Miller's *Tropic of Cancer* of obscenity charges and holds that only works "utterly without redeeming value" could legally be banned). It would prove to be the last time a work of literature was prosecuted on obscenity charges in the United States.

Burroughs, by writing *Naked Lunch* and then winning the landmark case, subverted censorship as surely as he subverted the art of writing. Novelist J.G. Ballard believes Burroughs was "very much aware of the way in which language could be manipulated to mean absolutely the opposite of what it seems to mean. But that's something he shared with George Orwell. He was always trying to go through the screen of language to find some sort of truth that lay on the other side."

"Artists to my mind are the real architects of change," said Burroughs, "and not the political legislators who implement change after the fact." ⧉

1965 Bob Dylan goes electric.

1965 District 1199 becomes first union to oppose the Vietnam War.

1965 Large-scale racial riots in Detroit.

1965 Lt. Henry Howe becomes first soldier court-martialed for protesting against the Vietnam War.

1965 A Students for a Democratic Society (SDS) leaflet reads: "What kind of America is it whose response to poverty and oppression in Vietnam is napalm and defoliation? Whose response to poverty and oppression in Mississippi is silence?"

33
LENNY BRUCE DIES FOR OUR SINS

I'm a surgeon with a scalpel for false values.
— **Lenny Bruce (1926-1966)**

"Lenny Bruce was a revolutionary comedy figure because he brought honesty into a form which previously had been little more than an empty crowd-pleasing truth," says George Carlin, "and he took it down the path that led to acceptance of the complete English language in his performance."

To say Bruce revolutionized comedy is putting it rather mildly. His impact extended beyond mere entertainment to alter American culture. Perhaps the single greatest indicator of his uniqueness lies in the fact that many of his classic stand-up bits no longer are funny. His primary topics —

religion, politics, sex — are hardly taboo anymore (thanks, in part, to Bruce) and thus his scathing attacks seem tame by today's standards.

Not so in the early 1960s when Bruce faced the repressive wrath of state power. As a former assistant district attorney admitted some 30 years after Bruce's death, "He was prosecuted because of his words. He didn't harm anybody; he didn't commit an assault; he didn't steal; he didn't engage in any conduct, which directly harmed someone else. So, therefore, he was punished, first and foremost, because of the words he used... We drove him into poverty and used the law to kill him."

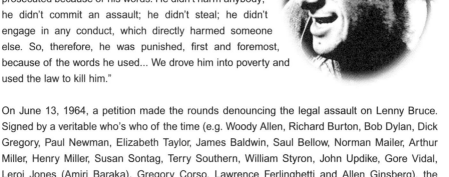

On June 13, 1964, a petition made the rounds denouncing the legal assault on Lenny Bruce. Signed by a veritable who's who of the time (e.g. Woody Allen, Richard Burton, Bob Dylan, Dick Gregory, Paul Newman, Elizabeth Taylor, James Baldwin, Saul Bellow, Norman Mailer, Arthur Miller, Henry Miller, Susan Sontag, Terry Southern, William Styron, John Updike, Gore Vidal, Leroi Jones (Amiri Baraka), Gregory Corso, Lawrence Ferlinghetti and Allen Ginsberg), the petition read, in part:

Lenny Bruce is a popular and controversial performer in the field of social satire in the tradition of Swift, Rabelais, and Twain. Although Bruce makes use of the

vernacular in his night-club performances, he does so within the context of his satirical intent and not to arouse the prurient interests of his listeners. It is up to the audience to determine what is offensive to them; it is not a function of the police department of New York or any other city to decide what adult private citizens may or may not hear.

Within two years, the battle had claimed Bruce. He was found dead in his apartment… never to witness the enduring effect of his efforts. "The greatest gift I derived from knowing him and his work was the importance of honesty, in the words and on the stage," Carlin states. "Lenny made being full of shit old-fashioned."

Or, as Lenny himself explained: "Take away the right to say fuck and you take away the right to say fuck the government." ⛢

TIMELINE:

1965 *The Autobiography of Malcolm X* is published.

1965 Six days of racial riots in Watts.

1966 After 25 years of use by the CIA, LSD is outlawed.

1966 SNCC declares: "We maintain that our country's cry of 'preserve freedom in the world' is a hypocritical mask behind which it squashed liberation movements which are not bound and refuse to be bound by the expedience of the United States' Cold War policy."

34
MUHAMMAD ALI SAYS "NO" TO THE MILITARY DRAFT

Man, I ain't got no quarrel with them Vietcong.
— **Muhammad Ali**

Muhammad Ali (b. 1942) could have made it into this book for a dozen reasons but his willingness to risk all he fought so hard to attain is perhaps his greatest legacy… and the most commonly ignored episode of his long, storied life.

"Ali has been absorbed by the establishment as a legend — a harmless icon," says Dave Zirin. "There is barely a trace left of the controversial truth: There has never been an athlete more reviled by the mainstream press, more persecuted by the U.S. government or more defiantly beloved throughout the world than Muhammad Ali."

The battles with Sonny Liston, Joe Frazier, George Foreman, and Ken Norton remain part of his legend. His rhyming speech, shuffling feet, rope-a-dope, and his eventual decline and rebirth as a sanitized hero — these are common knowledge. Speeches like this have been erased from the public record:

Why should they ask me to put on a uniform and go 10,000 miles from home and drop bombs and bullets on Brown people in Vietnam while so-called Negro people in Louisville are treated like dogs and denied simple human rights? No I'm not

going 10,000 miles from home to help murder and burn another poor nation simply to continue the domination of white slave masters of the darker people the world over. This is the day when such evils must come to an end. I have been warned that to take such a stand would cost me millions of dollars. But I have said it once and I will say it again. The real enemy of my people is here. I will not disgrace my religion, my people or myself by becoming a tool to enslave those who are fighting for their own justice, freedom and equality… If I thought the war was going to bring freedom and equality to 22 million of my people they wouldn't have to draft me, I'd join tomorrow. I have nothing to lose by standing up for my beliefs. So I'll go to jail, so what? We've been in jail for 400 years.

On June 19, 1967, an all-white jury in Houston found Muhammad Ali guilty for refusing to submit to the military draft. Although the standard sentence for such a charge was 18 months, Ali was given 5 years, his passport was confiscated, and he was stripped of the heavyweight title… eventually leading to three-and-a-half years of inactivity in the prime of his athletic life. All because he stood up for what he believed in.

Ali was roasted by the American press but his stance had immediate global impact.

"When Ali refused to take that symbolic step forward everyone knew about it moments later," said civil rights leader, Julian Bond. "You could hear people talking about it on street corners. It was on everybody's lips. People who had never thought about the war — black and white — began to think it through because of Ali."

Anti-war activist Daniel Berrigan added, "It was a major boost to an antiwar movement that was very white. He was not an academic, or a bohemian or a clergyman. He couldn't be dismissed as cowardly."

"Ali's refusal to fight in Vietnam was front-page news all over the world," Zirin writes. "In Guyana there was a picket of support in front of the U.S. embassy. In Karachi, young Pakistanis fasted. And there was a mass demonstration in Cairo."

Even Martin Luther King, Jr. spoke out in solidarity, declaring: "Like Muhammad Ali puts it, we are all — black and brown and poor — victims of the same system of oppression."

Sports fans like to play "what if?" when it comes to the time Ali was out of the ring at the height of his fighting powers… but his sacrifice served a far greater purpose than accolades or title belts.

As Ali explained during his exile: "I'm expected to go overseas to help free people in South Vietnam and at the same time my people here are being brutalized, hell no! I would like to say to those of you who think I have lost so much, I have gained everything. I have peace of heart; I have a clear, free conscience. And I am proud. I wake up happy, I go to bed happy, and if I go to jail I'll go to jail happy." ▢

TIMELINE:

1967 Jimi Hendrix plays the Monterey Pop Festival.

1967 Martin Luther King says: "When machines and computers, profit motives and property rights, are considered more important than people, the giant triplet of racism, extreme materialism, and militarism are incapable of being conquered."

35
CESAR CHAVEZ, UFW, AND THE GRAPE BOYCOTT

Here's some food for thought: In the late 1960s, thanks to Cesar Chavez (1927-1993) and the United Farm Workers (UFW), deciding whether or not to buy grapes was a political act.

Chavez was born in Arizona and migrated to California with his family… who worked the fields from Brawley to Oxnard, Atascadero, Gonzales, King City, Salinas, McFarland, Delano, Wasco, Selma, Kingsburg, and Mendota. The quiet man who lived in a barrio called *Sal Si Puedes* ("Get Out If You Can") knew firsthand of the injustices imposed upon the migrant workers — workers who had been trying to organize for a century. He and others like Dolores Huerta fought back… not with violence, but with the formation of the National Farm Workers Association (later to become the UFW) in 1962.

Three years after its establishment, the UFW struck against grape growers around Delano, California… a long, bitter, and frustrating struggle that appeared impossible to resolve until

Chavez hit upon the idea of a national boycott. Trusting in the average person's ability to connect with those in need, Chavez and the UFW brought their plight — and a lesson in social justice — into homes from coast-to-coast, and Americans responded.

"By 1970, the grape boycott was an unqualified success," writes Marc Grossman of *Stone Soup*. "Bowing to pressure from the boycott, grape growers at long last signed union contracts, granting workers human dignity and a more livable wage."

Chavez is perhaps best known for the grape boycott, but in line with his collective soul, he was always the first to admit that it was not his idea. In fact, he was initially against the boycott until his co-workers explained that the best method was not to boycott individual labels, but all grapes. In this way, the grapes became the label itself.

Through hunger strikes, imprisonment, abject poverty for himself and his large family, racist and corrupt judges, exposure to dangerous pesticides, and even assassination plots, Chavez remained true to the cause and to the non-violent methods he espoused. Even when threatened with physical harm, the furthest Chavez and his comrades would go is deterrence.

Once in 1966, when Teamster goons began to rough up Chavez's picketeers, a bit of labor solidarity solved the problem without violence. William Kircher, the AFL-CIO director of organization, called Paul Hall, president of the International Seafarers Union.

"Within hours," writes David Goodwin in *Cesar Chavez: Hope for the People*, "Hall sent a carload of the biggest sailors that had ever put to sea to march with the strikers on the picket lines… There followed afterward no further physical harassment."

This peaceful yet strong dedication garnered the attention of another non-violent struggle being waged at the time as Student Non-violent Coordinating Committee (SNCC) workers took some time from the civil rights movement to head west and help out. They were joined by members of the Free Speech Movement from Berkeley to form a powerful multi-ethnic coalition.

"The fight for equality must be fought on many fronts — in urban slums, in the sweat shops of the factories and fields," said Martin Luther King, Jr. in a telegram to Chavez after a UFW electoral victory. "Our separate struggles are really one — a struggle for freedom, for dignity and for humanity. You and your valiant fellow workers have demonstrated your commitment to righting grievous wrongs forced upon exploited people. We are together with you in spirit and in determination that our dreams for a better tomorrow will be realized."

The roots of Chavez's effectiveness lay in his ability to connect on a human level. When asked: "What accounts for all the affection and respect so many farm workers show you in public?", Cesar replied: "The feeling is mutual."

"He never owned a house," says Grossman. "He never earned more than $6,000 a year. When he died… he left no money for his family. Yet more than 40,000 people marched behind the plain pine casket at his funeral, honoring the more than 40 years he spent struggling to improve the lives of farm workers." ⊄

1968 Philip and Daniel Berrigan are arrested for destroying Selective Service files in Catonsville, MD.

1968 James Brown releases "Say it Loud — I'm Black and I'm Proud."

1968 Protests at the Democratic Convention.

1968 William Kunstler, modern day attorney for the damned, defends the Chicago Seven.

Patriot Words...

If the test of patriotism comes only by reflexively falling into lockstep behind the leader whenever the flag is waved, then what we have is a formula for dictatorship, not democracy.

— Michael Parenti

36
HUGH THOMPSON GETS IN THE LINE OF FIRE

Thompson and his crew watched as an infantry officer, wearing a captain's bars on his helmet, came up to the woman, prodded her with his foot, and then killed her.
— From *Four Hours at My Lai*, by Michael Bilton and Kevin Sim

Hugh Clowers Thompson, Jr. (b. 1943) wanted to fly choppers so badly that after a four-year stint in the Navy, he left his wife and two sons behind to re-up into the Army and train as a helicopter pilot. Thompson arrived in Vietnam on December 27, 1967 and quickly earned a reputation as "an exceptional pilot who took danger in his stride." In their book, *Four Hours at My Lai*, Michael Bilton and Kevin Sim also describe Hugh Thompson as a "very moral man. He was absolutely strict about opening fire only on clearly defined targets." On the morning of March 16, 1968 Thompson's sense of virtue would be put to the test.

Flying in his H-23 observation chopper, the 25-year-old Thompson used green smoke to mark wounded people on the ground in and around My Lai. Upon returning a short while later after refueling, he found that the wounded he saw earlier were now dead. Thompson's gunner, Lawrence Colburn, averted his gaze from the gruesome sight.

After bringing the chopper down to a standstill hover, Thompson and his crew came upon a young woman they had previously marked with smoke. As they watched, a U.S. soldier, wearing captain's bars, "prodded her with his foot, and then killed her."

Unbeknownst to Thompson at that point, more than 560 Vietnamese had already been slaughtered by Lt. William Calley's Charlie Company. All Thompson knew for sure was that the U.S. troops he then saw pursuing civilians had to be stopped.

Bravely landing his helicopter between the charging GIs and the fleeing villagers, Thompson ordered Colburn to turn his machine gun on the American soldiers if they tried to shoot the unarmed men, women, and children. Thompson then stepped out of the chopper into the combat zone and coaxed the frightened civilians from the bunker they were hiding in. With tears streaming down his face, he evacuated them to safety on his H-23.

Officially termed an "incident" (as a opposed to a "massacre") My Lai has been widely accepted as an aberration. While the record of U.S. war crimes in Southeast Asia is far too lengthy to detail here, it's clear that was not the case. In fact, on the very same day that Lt. Calley entered into infamy (he later explained: "We weren't there to kill human beings, really. We were there to kill ideology"), another company entered My Khe, a sister subhamlet of My Lai. That visit was described in *Fifth Estate* as such: "In this 'other massacre,' members of this separate company piled up a body count of perhaps a hundred peasants — My Khe was smaller than My Lai — 'flattened the village' by dynamite and fire, and then threw handfuls of straw on corpses. The next morning, this company moved on down the Batangan Peninsula by the South China Sea, burning every hamlet they came to, killing water buffalo, pigs, chickens, ducks, and destroying crops. As one of the My Khe veterans said later, 'what we were doing was being done all over.' Said another: 'We were out there having a good time. It was sort of like being in a shooting gallery.'"

Colonel Oran Henderson, charged with covering up the My Lai killings, put it succinctly in 1971: "Every unit of brigade size has its My Lai hidden someplace."

But not every unit had a Hugh Thompson. ⌘

TIMELINE:
1968 Shirley Chisholm becomes the first African-American woman elected to Congress.
1969 Kurt Vonnegut writes *Slaughterhouse Five*.
1969 *Easy Rider* is released.

37
AMERICAN INDIANS OCCUPY ALCATRAZ ISLAND

Until the federal penitentiary was closed in 1963, Alcatraz Island was a place most folks tried to leave. On Nov. 20, 1969, the island's image underwent a drastic makeover. That was the day thousands of American Indians began an occupation that would last until June 11, 1971.

The 1973 armed occupation of Wounded Knee along with the siege at the Pine Ridge Reservation one year later (which led directly to the incarceration of Leonard Peltier) are etched deeper in the public consciousness in terms of recent Indian history, but it was the Alcatraz Island occupation that ushered in a new era of Native American activism.

"The occupiers," writes Ben Winton in the Fall 1999 issue of *Native Peoples* magazine, "were an unlikely mix of Indian college activists, families with children fresh off reservations and urban dwellers disenchanted with what they called the U.S. government's economic, social and political neglect."

"We hold The Rock," proclaimed Richard Oakes, a Mohawk from New York. Oakes became the occupiers' spokesman… and his words became their motto. "The occupation of Alcatraz was about human rights," said Winton. "It was an effort to restore the dignity of the more than 554 American Indian nations in the United States."

Over the course of the occupation, over 5600 American Indians took part — some for a day, some for the entire 18 months. Twenty-three year-old John Trudell, a Santee Sioux from San Bernardino, California heard about the occupation, packed a sleeping bag, and headed to Frisco. "He became the voice of Radio Free Alcatraz, a pirate station that broadcast from the island with the help of local stations" explains Winton. "When he hit the airwaves, the response was often overwhelming. Boxes of food and money poured in from everywhere — from rock groups such as The Grateful Dead and Creedence Clearwater Revival (who staged a concert on a boat off Alcatraz and then donated the boat), Jane Fonda, Marlon Brando, city politicians, and everyday folks." For the first time in modern American history, the plight of Native Americans was making headlines.

The fledgling American Indian Movement (AIM) visited the occupiers and soon began a series of their own occupations across America. AIM would soon become a powerful multi-tribal protest organization… just one of the many important outcomes of the Alcatraz takeover.

"Despite its chaos and factionalism, the event resulted in major benefits for American Indians," Winton states. "Years later, Brad Patterson, a top aide to President Richard Nixon, cited at least ten major policy and law shifts." Some of those policy shifts include:

• Passage of the Indian Self Determination and Education Act
• Revision of the Johnson O'Malley Act to better educate Indians
• Passage of the Indian Financing Act and the Indian Health Act
• Creation of an Assistant Interior Secretary post for Indian Affairs

Even today, Alcatraz Island remains part of Native American culture. Every November since 1975, on what is called "Un-Thanksgiving Day," Indians gather on the island to honor the occupation and those who continue to fight today. ⎔

TIMELINE:

1969 The concert at Woodstock.

1969 The Haymarket Square statue, a tribute to seven cops killed in 1886, is blown up by the Weathermen.

38
TOMMIE SMITH AND JOHN CARLOS
RAISE THEIR FISTS

They stood barefoot on the medal podium at the Mexico City 1968 Olympics, beads dangling from their necks. As America's national anthem commenced, sprinters Tommie Smith (b. 1944) — the son of a migrant worker — and Harlem's John Carlos (b. 1945) raised their black-gloved fists in the air.

Dave Zirin calls it, "arguably the most enduring image in sports history," but hastens to add, "the image has stood the test of time, the politics that led to that moment has been cast aside by capitalism's commitment to political amnesia; its political teeth extracted."

"I didn't do what I did as an athlete; I raised my voice in protest as a man," John Carlos told Zirin in 2003. The protest voiced by Carlos and Smith provoked a firestorm as the International Olympic Committee (IOC) not only forced the U.S. Olympic Committee to withdraw the two world class sprinters from the upcoming relays, the IOC had them expelled from the U.S. Olympic team.

"We didn't come up there with any bombs," says Carlos. "We were trying to wake the country up and wake the world up too."

Contrary to Rosa Parks-like rumors, Carlos and Smith were not acting alone or spontaneously. Teammates at San Jose State College, they had both been involved in a planned Olympic boycott by black athletes. "In the fall of 1967 amateur black athletes formed Olympic Project for Human Rights (OPHR) to organize a boycott of the 1968 Olympics in Mexico City," Zirin explains. The OPHR founding statement read, in part:

We must no longer allow this country to use a few so-called Negroes to point out to the world how much progress she has made in solving her racial problems when the oppression of Afro-Americans is greater than it ever was. We must no longer allow the sports world to pat itself on the back as a citadel of racial justice when the racial injustices of the sports world are infamously legendary... any black person who allows himself to be used in the above matter is a traitor because he allows racist whites the luxury of resting assured that those black people in the ghettos are there because that is where they want to be. So we ask why should we run in Mexico only to crawl home?

The OPHR also demanded the restoration of Muhammad Ali's heavyweight title (stripped due to his resistance to the military draft), the removal of white supremacist Avery Brundage as head of the United States Olympic Committee, and the "disinviting" of two apartheid states, South Africa and Rhodesia.

The IOC made the gesture of conceding on the third demand… a move that cleverly blunted the threat of a boycott. Carlos and Smith were far from satisfied. Thus, on the second day of the Games, when Smith set a world record in the 200 meters and Carlos placed third, they had a stage on which to stand barefoot.

"We wanted the world to know that in Mississippi, Alabama, Tennessee, South Central Los Angeles, Chicago, that people were still walking back and forth in poverty without even the necessary clothes to live," says Carlos. "We have kids that don't have shoes even today. It's not like the powers that be can't provide these things. They can send a spaceship to the moon, or send a probe to Mars, yet they can't give shoes? They can't give health care? I'm just not naive enough to accept that."

The beads around their necks were for "those individuals that were lynched, or killed that no one said a prayer for, that were hung tarred. It was for those thrown off the side of the boats in the Middle Passage."

Again, contrary to whitewashed history, the two men were not acting without support. "When the silver medalist, a runner from Australia named Peter Norman saw what was happening, he ran into the stands to grab an OPHR patch off a supporters' chest to show his solidarity on the medal stand," Zirin adds.

As the American flag began its ascent up the flagpole and the opening notes of the "Star Spangled Banner" played, Carlos and Smith stood barefoot with heads bowed and fists raised in a black power salute. The photographs of that moment rival any pre-staged Iwo Jima flag-raising. The fallout — both positive and negative — was instantaneous.

"They violated one of the basic principles of the Olympic Games: that politics play no part whatsoever in them," Brundage declared. The *Los Angeles Times* called the raised fists a "Nazi-like salute."

Wyomia Tyus, anchor of the women's gold medal winning 4x100 team, dedicated her team's gold medal to Carlos and Smith, while the all white crew team issued a public statement announcing their "moral commitment to support our black teammates in their efforts to dramatize the injustices and inequities which permeate our society."

"It was a watershed moment of resistance," writes Zirin. "But Carlos and Smith are not merely creatures of nostalgia. As we build resistance today to war, theirs is a living history we should celebrate."

"It's not something I can lay on my shelf and forget about," concludes Tommie Smith. "My heart and soul are still on that team, and I still believe everything we were trying to fight for in 1968 has not been resolved and will be part of our future." ⛎

TIMELINE:
1970 The Health Revolutionary Unity Movement (HRUM), organized in part by the Young Lords, takes over the old Lincoln Hospital to publicize the poor treatment of the underprivileged. Many clerical workers, nurses, and doctors stayed in the hospital during the occupation to show their solidarity.

39
STONEWALL

Despite the commodification of homosexuality through television shows like *The L Word* or *Queer Eye for the Straight Guy*, America has long been and remains in many ways a homophobic society. As is the case for all oppressed groups, progress, reform, and eventual acceptance begins with taking a stand against discrimination. For the gay rights movement, that stand was symbolically taken on Friday evening, June 27, 1969 in what has become known as "Stonewall."

It wasn't as if the struggle for gay rights did not exist before Stonewall (e.g. The Mattachine Society and The Daughters of Bilitis), but in the summer of 1969, let's just say the movement got militant.

Police raids on gay bars were not uncommon in the pre-Stonewall era. Patrons were subjected to fines for "indecency" and often found their names published in newspapers as a result. The revolutionary tenor of the 1960s helped change some of that, but New York City Mayor John Lindsay was in the middle of a difficult campaign run and the Stonewall Inn was operating without a liquor license and with alleged ties to organized crime. It seemed like a good place for a high profile law and order photo op.

At 1:20 AM, later than the usual raid — which obviously increased the chances of intoxicated patrons — eight officers from New York's First Precinct entered the bar. Only one of the cops was in uniform. Arrests were made but precisely how the riot began is still subject to debate. One story has a drag queen taking a swing at a police officer after being prodded by his nightstick, while others say it was a lesbian who struggled as a cop tried to get her through the crowd to his squad car that inspired the resistance. The most dramatic account has a burly Stonewaller tossing a metal garbage can filled with empty liquor bottles through a police car window.

Whichever story you prefer, what happened next is not in doubt. Stonewall patrons said no. They attacked the eight cops, driving them back into the bar, where they sought refuge. The angry throng laid siege to the bar as NYPD reinforcements arrived on the scene. In no time, a crowd, estimated at over 2000, was waging a pitched battle with more than 400 cops. The riot lasted all night and less massive skirmishes occurred for the following two nights. Arrests and injuries were numerous. Mayor Lindsay had his photo op… but it was not what he had bargained for.

The impact was immediate and enduring. Gay activists, energized by the event, stood alongside blacks, women, college students, and anti-war protestors in demanding an end to oppression. Hundreds and then thousands of gay and lesbian organizations sprung up across the U.S. and, by 1987, the movement was able to mobilize 600,000 people to march on Washington, D.C., demanding equality. ⛋

TIMELINE:

1970 National Guard kills four Kent State students and two Jackson State students.

1970 Black Panther leader Huey P. Newton writes to South Vietnam's National Liberation Front (NLF) and offers to send a battalion of Panthers to help fight American invaders.

1971 Abbie Hoffman writes *Steal This Book*.

1971 1200 prisoners seize control of the maximum-security facility at Attica.

40
ANGELA'S AFRO

Revolution is a serious thing, the most serious thing about a revolutionary's life. When one commits oneself to the struggle, it must be for a lifetime.
— **Angela Davis (b. 1944)**

There she stood: proud, defiant, black, and female… fist in the air and the biggest damn Afro you could imagine. Angela Davis broke the mold. Preconceptions about women, about blacks, about communists, about dissent — they were all challenged both in mainstream society and in the radical movements of the time.

Best known for her involvement in the Black Panthers, Davis was also active with Student Non-violent Coordinating Committee (SNCC). Pronounced "snick," SNCC was created in 1960 on the campus of Shaw University in Raleigh, North Carolina, after a group of black college students refused to leave a Woolworth's lunch counter where they were denied service.

"Davis joined the Communist Party in 1968 and suffered discrimination like many blacks during the late 1960s for her personal political beliefs and commitment to revolutionary ideals," says Alex Burns of Disinfo.com. "Despite her qualifications and excellent teaching record, the California Board of Regents refused to renew her appointment as a philosophy lecturer in 1970."

That was the year Davis was placed on the FBI's Ten Most Wanted List, forcing her underground. After her eventual arrest and a consequent international "Free Angela Davis" campaign, her trial was news across the globe.

This series of events grew out of Davis' work to free a group of African-American prisoners held in California's Soledad Prison. "She befriended George Jackson, one of the prisoners," says Burns. "On August 7, 1970, during an abortive escape and kidnap attempt from Marin County's Hall of Justice, the trial judge and three people were killed, including Jackson's brother Jonathan. Although not at the crime scene, Davis was implicated when police claimed that the guns used had been registered in her name."

Eighteen months later, Angela Davis — backed by massive global support and buoyed by her resolute pursuit of justice — was cleared of all charges by an all white jury. She promptly re-doubled her efforts and dedicated herself to challenging the prison-industrial complex. Davis resumed teaching and penned several books, including *If They Come In The Morning* (1971), *Angela Davis: An Autobiography* (1974), *Women, Race & Class* (1981), *Women, Race and Politics* (1989), *Blues Legacies & Black Feminism* (1999), *The Angela Y. Davis Reader* (1999), and *Are Prisons Obsolete?* (2003).

"Her revolutionary politics and academic writings provide a link from 1960s groups like the Black Panthers to contemporary cases including Leonard Peltier and Mumia Abu Jamal," Burns concludes. "Ultimately Davis represents a revitalizing force in New Left politics (she was at the forefront of Gulf War protests in the United States that were censored by the mainstream media) and individual life-affirming cultural studies (particularly blues and hip-hop music)."

In 1970, then-Governor of California Ronald Reagan publicly vowed that Davis would never teach in that state again. Reagan is dead and buried while Angela Davis is inspiring a new generation toward critical thought as a professor in the History of Consciousness Department at University of California, Santa Cruz… in California. ▯

TIMELINE:

1971 14,000 are arrested at an anti-war protest in Washington, D.C., the largest mass arrest in U.S. history.

1971 Frank Serpico reveals corruption in the NYPD.

1971 Edwin Starr sings: "War, what is it good for? Absolutely nothing."

1972 Gloria Steinem founds *Ms.* magazine.

41
CURT FLOOD CHALLENGES BASEBALL'S RESERVE CLAUSE

There is no Hall of Fame for people like Curt.

— **Marvin Miller, former executive director of the Major League Players Association**

By 1969, Curt Flood (1938-1997) had compiled some rather impressive career stats as a member of the St. Louis Cardinals: a three-time All-Star center fielder with seven Gold Gloves, he batted more than .300 six times. But when the 31-year-old Flood was dealt to the Philadelphia Phillies before the 1970 season, he did something that left an indelible mark on the sports landscape: he challenged baseball's "reserve clause." This was the standard contract clause that essentially bound baseball players to one team forever… one year at a time.

Why would Flood risk his $100,000 salary in such a challenge? One reason would have been his opinion of Philadelphia as a racist town… Flood called it "the nation's northernmost southern city." More important to the open-minded athlete, however, was the way in which the reserve clause made him feel like a piece of property.

"I'm a child of the sixties, I'm a man of the sixties," Flood explained. "During that period of time this country was coming apart at the seams. We were in Southeast Asia. Good men were dying for America and for the Constitution. In the southern part of the United States we were marching for civil rights and Dr. King had been assassinated, and we lost the Kennedys. And to think that merely because I was a professional baseball player, I could ignore what was going on outside the walls of Busch Stadium was truly hypocrisy and now I found that all of those rights that these great Americans were dying for, I didn't have in my own profession."

For 18 months, Curt Flood put his career on hold and pursued the case all the way up to the Supreme Court… which upheld baseball's exemption from antitrust statutes. Although Flood's legal efforts effectively ended his major league career, they were not in vain. Within three years, the reserve clause was struck down and the era of free agency was ushered in.

While it's difficult to reconcile Flood's stance with what free agency has since become, his sacrifice in the name of economic freedom was nothing short of a one-man revolution. Unfortunately, those who gained the most from Flood's defiance have little sense of revolution… or history. When Flood died of throat cancer in 1997 at the age of 59, baseball's multi-millionaires never paid proper respect.

"I'm sorry that so many of the young players who made millions, who benefited from his fight, are not here," former player Tito Fuentes commented at Flood's memorial service. "They should be here."

Marvin Miller, former executive director of the Major League Players Association, was left to put it in perspective: "At the time Curt Flood decided to challenge baseball's reserve clause, he was perhaps the sport's premier center fielder. And yet he chose to fight an injustice, knowing that even if by some miracle he won, his career as a professional player would be over. At no time did he waver in his commitment and determination. He had experienced something that was inherently unfair and was determined to right the wrong, not so much for himself, but for those who would come after him. Few praised him for this, then or now."

In a time when everyone seems to want to "be like Mike," we could use a few more Curts. ⌷

TIMELINE:

1972 Bob Marley and the Wailers sign with Island Records.

1972 Marvin Gaye releases "What's Goin' On."

1973 The American Psychiatric Association removes homosexuality from its official list of mental disorders.

1973 American Indian Movement occupation of Wounded Knee.

42
DANIEL ELLSBERG LEAKS THE PENTAGON PAPERS

The Pentagon Papers are mesmerizing, not as documentation of the history of the U.S. war in Indochina, but as insight into the minds of the men who planned and executed it. It's fascinating to be privy to the ideas that were being tossed around, the suggestions that were made, the proposals that were put forward.

— Arundhati Roy

On June 13, 1971, the *New York Times* published an article by Neil Sheehan called, "Vietnam Archive: Pentagon Study Traces 3 Decades of Growing U.S. Involvement." It was the first installment of a 7000-page document that came to be known as the "Pentagon Papers." How important was the public airing of a secret government study of decision-making about the Vietnam War? None other than Henry Kissinger labeled the man who leaked that study — Daniel Ellsberg (b. 1931) — "the most dangerous man in America."

Author H. Bruce Franklin called Ellsberg, "That young man with boundless promise who graduated third in his Harvard class of 1,147 in 1952, when America too seemed boundlessly promising." An officer in the U.S. Marines, a Cold War theoretician for the Pentagon, Franklin explains that Ellsberg was "not content with planning wars for others to fight and defending the Vietnam War on college campuses, (so he) volunteered in 1965 to go to Vietnam" where he "displayed such personal bravery in combat that some, such as his present biographer, claim he must have been suicidal."

All that changed in 1969 when Ellsberg discovered that President Richard Nixon was "the fifth president in a row now… choosing to prolong the war in vain hopes that he might get a better outcome than he could achieve if he'd just negotiated his way out." Nixon, like those who came before him, would not accept anything that even looked like defeat and nothing would change his or his handlers' minds.

"That meant that if his decision was going to be changed — and because I cared about Vietnam and this country, I felt quite urgently that I wanted the United States to stop bombing them and stop killing Vietnamese — the pressure would have to come from outside the executive branch," explained Ellsberg. "Reading the Pentagon Papers and reflecting on Vietnam revealed to me (that) you could do more for the country outside the executive branch."

Knowing full well his actions might result in his spending the rest of his days behind bars, Ellsberg leaked the document to the *Times*. The Nixon administration knew what the impact of this leak might be.

"To the ordinary guy, all this is a bunch of gobbledygook," H.R. Haldeman told Nixon on June 14. "But out of the gobbledygook comes a very clear thing: you can't trust the government; you can't believe what they say; and you can't rely on their judgment. And the implicit infallibility of presidents, which has been an accepted thing in America, is badly hurt by this, because it shows that people do things the president wants to do even though it's wrong, and the president can be wrong."

Further demonstrating just how wrong a president can be, Nixon ordered the *Times* to halt publication. This was done through a temporary restraining order from federal district court. When the government and the *Times* tangled, the *Washington Post* entered the fray by publishing parts of the Pentagon Papers on June 18, 1971... this despite a personal plea from Assistant U.S. Attorney General William Rehnquist (now Chief Justice of the U.S. Supreme Court).

Within two weeks, the case reached the Supreme Court, where, in a 6-3 decision, the government was told it could not block publication of the Pentagon Papers. Two days earlier, Ellsberg had been charged with theft, conspiracy, and espionage, but Nixon's ability to be wrong knew no bounds. In September 1971, the president had the infamous G. Gordon Liddy and E. Howard Hunt break into Ellsberg's psychiatrist's office in an effort to dig up dirt on the whistleblower. This break-in became public knowledge during the Watergate scandal (along with an alleged plot to assassinate Ellsberg) and all charges were eventually dropped.

Ellsberg's courage had opened the eyes of a nation blinded by wartime propaganda. As the wounded marine-turned-author W.D. Ehrhart wrote in his memoir, *Passing Time*, about reading the Pentagon Papers: "Page after endless page of it. Vile. Immoral. Despicable. Obscene… I'd been a fool, ignorant and naive. A sucker. For such men, I had become a murderer. For such men, I had forfeited my honor, my self-respect, and my humanity. For such men, I had been willing to lay down my life."

To that, Daniel Ellsberg said: Not in my name. ⚲

TIMELINE:

1973 Bruce Lee goes from Asian-American sidekick (Kato) to Asian-American hero in *Enter the Dragon*.

1973 *Roe v. Wade*.

1973 Billie Jean King defeats Bobby Riggs.

1975 Peter Singer writes *Animal Liberation*.

43
CHARLES BUKOWSKI QUITS
HIS JOB AT THE POST OFFICE

"It began as a mistake." With that audacious opening line does Charles Bukowski (1920-1994) launch his first novel, *Post Office* (1971). Others had challenged the vaunted American work ethic before… but none with the style and vengeance of the man they called Hank.

In the U.S., the topic of work infiltrates most aspects of our life. Consider the most common question we're asked from the time we're old enough to understand it: What are you going to be when you grow up? The unspoken assumption in that question, of course, is that the child or teen on the receiving end is nothing now… but he or she will be something when he or she spends 8-10 hours a day in a cubicle crunching numbers under artificial light to the sound of Muzak. Breaking free from this cookie-cutter formula has become increasingly difficult as one's perceived worth is usually synonymous with one's earning power and material consumption.

Bukowski unapologetically mocked and deconstructed this American edifice, writing in *Post Office*: "Any damn fool can beg up some kind of job; it takes a wise man to make it without working."

And he knew of what he wrote. To support his writing, Bukowski toiled in a wide range of jobs including dishwasher, truck driver and loader, mail carrier, guard, gas station attendant, stock boy, warehouse worker, shipping clerk, parking lot attendant, Red Cross orderly, and elevator operator. Other venues of employment included a dog biscuit factory, a slaughterhouse, a cake and cookie factory, and the New York City subways where he hung posters. Then, of course, came the years at the post office… the years he chronicles in his first novel.

"You won't find Bukowski on most English professors' reading lists, because Bukowski writes too clearly," says novelist Anis Shivani. "It isn't possible to fudge his message to make bourgeois life look all right, after all."

"Bukowski wrote about men and women as beaten down as a crunched beer can, about endurance, rage, longing, sex and, mostly, about himself," says William Booth, a *Washington Post* staff writer. "He was a bestseller in Brazil; his poetry is taught to high school students in France; in the United States, in his day, he was a symbol of rebellion."

That rebellion lives on every time a store has to shelve *Post Office* and other Buk books behind the counter to prevent shoplifting. Hank's books, it seems, are the most commonly pilfered. As a bookstore owner explained: "Bukowski was an anti-establishment writer, he took a lot of risks and pretty much did whatever he wanted. Perhaps people consider stealing his books as an act of solidarity. Because of Bukowski's style, they most likely see it as okay to steal his books; it's a gesture against the establishment."

And it all began as a mistake. ▢

1974 Gill Scott-Heron sings: "The revolution will not be televised…. The revolution will be live."

1975 Philip Agee writes *CIA Diary: Inside the Company*.

1977 The Ramones release their self-titled debut album.

1979 Earth First! is formed.

44
PATTI SMITH USES ROCK AND ROLL LIKE A WEAPON

*When I entered rock 'n roll, I entered into it in a
political sort of way, not as a career.*

— Patti Smith (b. 1946)

I'm not talking here about the Patti Smith who stumped for John Kerry in 2004. This is all about the punk poetess whose first line in the first song on her first album was:

Jesus died for somebody's sins but not mine…

I'm talking about the Patti Smith described in 1975 by Charles Shaar Murray in NME as "an odd little waif figure in a grubby black suit and black satin shirt, so skinny that her clothes hang baggily all over her, with chopped-off black hair and a face like Keith Richards' kid sister would have if she'd gotten as wasted by age seventeen as Keith is now." This is about the rock revolutionary that Murray accused of having "an aura that'd probably show up under ultraviolet light. She can generate more intensity with a single movement of one hand than most rock performers can produce in an entire set."

"Rock 'n roll was revolutionary for me," Smith says. "Songs were weapons. People were afraid of rock music, they called it the Devil's music — and they were right! It was the music of the revolution. Rock's spiritual, political, and emotional content was stirring and important and it gave us strength."

"Patti kicked gender in the balls and made great rock 'n roll by following her own agenda, without falling into the role of the victim," Legs McNeil wrote in *Spin* magazine. "And in the process, Patti opened the doors for every woman who looked up on the stage and didn't imagine herself down on her knees blowing the rock god, but becoming one."

"To me, a rock 'n roll star wasn't all about lifestyle and record sales," says Smith. "It was… people who had something to say, who would excite and incite, who possessed both revolutionary and poetic powers."

To read Murray's take on a 1975 gig at CBGB's, you'd have to believe Smith had the whole "excite and incite" thing down. "Patti Smith embodied and equaled everybody that I've ever dug on a rock and roll stage," Murray wrote. "Patti Smith has always had the ability to create joy from despair and hope from fear," adds author Ron Jacobs. "One imagines this is what brought her to rock and roll."

"I wanted to be like Paul Revere," Smith told William S. Burroughs in 1979. "That was my whole thing. I wanted to be like Paul Revere. I didn't want to be a giant big hero; I didn't want to die for the cause. I didn't want to be a martyr. All that I wanted was for the people to fuckin' wake up."

If it's difficult for you to reconcile Patti Smith's revolutionary roots with her recent, more mainstream political efforts, well, so it is for Smith herself.

"That rock 'n roll has evolved into something else is everybody's fault," she says. "We all have to take responsibility. You can't say 'I had to do that, because the marketing people said to.' It's the artists' fault. It's MTV's fault. We're all guilty of forgetting what a great and powerful weapon rock 'n roll is." ⌻

TIMELINE:
1980 Howard Zinn writes *A People's History of the United States.*
1980 People for the Ethical Treatment of Animals (PETA) is founded.
1980s Environmental Liberation Front and Animal Liberation Front cells begin actions.

45
KEITH MCHENRY FORMS FOOD NOT BOMBS

*Food Not Bombs' central unifying principles are
a commitment to nonviolence, free unrestricted access to vegetarian food, and an honest
attempt to make decisions as a group without hierarchy.*
— **Keith McHenry (b. 1957)**

Created in Cambridge, Massachusetts in 1980, Food Not Bombs (FNB) is the brainchild of Keith McHenry and seven other activists. "We came out of the Clamshell Alliance," says McHenry, "[which was] trying to shut down Seabrook Nuclear Power Plant. It was a collection of mostly anarchists but also included Quakers and the Red Clams, who were socialists."

FNB is responsible for starting hundreds of autonomous chapters throughout the Americas, Europe, Asia and Australia… where food that would otherwise be thrown out is recovered and transformed into hot vegetarian meals that are then served to the homeless and at protests and other events. With roots in a variety of social causes, it's not surprising that McHenry describes the FNB project as essentially "the food wing of a movement that includes anti-authoritarian music, art, unlicensed radio, zines, squatting, needle exchange, bike and hemp liberation, info shops, computer networking, autonomous decentralized non-hierarchical organizing, consensus decision-making, and sharing a philosophy of tolerance, joy, and free expression."

By linking the national problem of homelessness with the larger issue of rampant militarism,

McHenry's goal is to address "the inhumane agenda of the government at both the personal and international levels" as a path towards beginning a nationwide debate. This goal is being aimed for not only with commitment and passion, but also with creativity… often in the face of massive police repression.

Members of the San Francisco FNB chapter have been arrested over 1,000 times. Their situation has reached the point where Amnesty International may adopt imprisoned FNB volunteers as "Prisoners of Conscience" and work for their unconditional release.

"From the very beginning," McHenry explains, "we saw all our street activity as theater." It is not uncommon at a FNB gathering or event to witness improvisational street theater depicting such scenarios as military types holding a bake sale to buy a B-1 bomber or a person dressed like a papier-mâché missile chasing another person dressed like a papier-mâché planet Earth, threatening to destroy it. Then, of course, there's always the opportunity to take the "tofu challenge," rather than the Pepsi challenge.

"The only limits to what kind of theater you present are your imagination and your pocketbook," he adds.

"The Food Not Bombs volunteers believe that it's not too late to help build an alternative to transnational corporate greed," says Keith. "People, through their actions, can change the political agenda."

FNB just celebrated its 25th anniversary promoting the concept that food is a right, not a privilege. ⵔ

TIMELINE:

1981 Mumia Abu Jamal receives a death sentence.

1985 Columbia University students occupy Hamilton Hall to demand South African divestment. Protests follow on 100 campuses, 27 schools divest within a year.

1986 Fairness and Accuracy in Reporting (FAIR) is founded.

1988 Noam Chomsky and Edward Herman write *Manufacturing Consent: The Political Economy of the Mass Media.*

Patriot Words...

Dissent, rebellion, and all-around hell-raising remain the true duty of patriots.

— Barbara Ehrenreich

46
JOHN ROBBINS MAKES ALL THE CONNECTIONS

Like so many other aspects of American life, we've relinquished control of our eating habits to the corporate pirates and their well-paid propagandists...and in the process, surrendered part of our humanity. Thanks to decades of indoctrination, eating animals is as "normal" as breathing while the consequent animal cruelty required to sustain this lifestyle is, at worst, considered a necessary evil on all sides of the political spectrum.

In a society crushed under the onerous weight of corporate dominance, eschewing the standard American meat- and dairy-based diet is indeed a radical act. John Robbins (b. 1947) turning his back on his family's Baskin-Robbins fortune to spread the word about veganism: well, that's downright revolutionary.

In 1987, Robbins began *Diet for a New America: How Your Food Choices Affect Your Health, Happiness, and the Future of Life on Earth* with this line: "I was born into the heart of the Great American Food Machine." For the next 400 or so pages, he connects the dots and peels away the thin veneer of normalcy as he explains how the purveyors of that machine "don't want you to know how the animals have lived whose flesh, milk, and eggs end up in your body." In his tender yet uncompromising style, Robbins demonstrates that "they" also "don't want you to know the health consequences of consuming the products of such a system, nor do they want you to know its environmental impact."

Robbins, however, wants us to know, and wants the world to know. "I'm letting the cat out of the bag," he announces. "I don't care about your profits. I care about your health, your well-being, and the welfare of our planet and all its creatures."

A health holocaust of preventable, degenerative diseases, mind-numbing animal cruelty, devastating, perhaps irreparable environmental damage, and corporate economics at its worst… these are just a taste of what the Standard American Diet (SAD) brings to the planet. Surrounded by global issues we often feel powerless to influence, *Diet for a New America* points readers toward a form of activism that is immediate and accessible to all. Robbins offers guidelines for each of us to make a difference at least three times a day.

"Few of us are aware that the act of eating can be a powerful statement of commitment to our well-being," writes Robbins, who has gone on to write several more influential books and create Earthsave International, "and at the very same time to the creation of a healthier habitat." Robbins believes (and does an effective job in making his readers believe) that once we "become aware of the impact of our food choices, we can never really forget."

Diet for a New America is nothing if not unforgettable. ♡

TIMELINE:
1988 AIDS Coalition to Unleash Power (ACT-UP) is founded.
1989 Ani DiFranco forms Righteous Babe Records.
1989 600,000 march in Washington, D.C. demanding choice on abortion.

47
PUBLIC ENEMY FIGHTS THE POWER

Elvis was a hero to most
But he never meant shit to me you see
Straight up racist that sucker was
Simple and plain
Motherfuck him and John Wayne
— "Fight the Power," Public Enemy (PE), 1989

"Although it never cracked the Top 40, Public Enemy's 'Fight the Power' became the soundtrack to 1989's summer of rage," writes Johnny Black in *Blender*. "That year, director Spike Lee released *Do the Right Thing*, a movie he wrote to portray the violence of the time — particularly the often fatal clashes between African-Americans and the New York Police Department."

The opening credits rolled, Rosie Perez danced, "Fight the Power" blared, and political hip-hop was now in everyone's face. "I didn't want to rap about 'I'm this or I'm that' all the time," explains PE's Chuck D. (b. 1960). "My focus was not on boasting about myself or battling brothers on the microphone. I wanted to rap about battling institutions, and bringing the condition of black people worldwide to a respectable level."

"Unabashedly political, 'Fight the Power' was confrontational in the way great rock has always been," Laura K. Warrell wrote in *Salon*. "It had the kind of irreverence that puts bands on FBI lists. 'Fight' demanded action and, as the band's most accessible hit, acted as the perfect summation of its ideology and sound. Every kid in America, white, black or brown, could connect to the song's uncompromising cultural critique, its invigoratingly danceable sound and its rallying call… By 1989, Public Enemy was more than a rap act, it was a social movement."

"Today's artists don't seem to know what real provocateurs like Public Enemy know: Shock is a short-lived effect that wears off quickly and has no real consequences," says Warrell. "Art can be relevant without being overtly political, but if there are no real motives or ideas behind shock, its images too often fall flat… When Public Enemy called us to battle, it revived the notion that it just might be possible to fight the system. At the very least, we knew it was necessary."

The release of "Fight the Power," says hip hop historian Nelson George, is one of the genre's top ten moments.

"As I've moved forward," Chuck D. says, "I've come to respect that record for what it meant. When you're doing it, you don't know what it's going to take on, and it came to mean a lot. If somebody keeps you from being as equal as everybody else or from having the freedom to contribute what you can to the world, you have to fight those powers as much as possible." ⛢

1990 Americans with Disabilities Act is signed.

1991 Kurt Cobain and Nirvana reinvigorate rock and roll.

1991 School of the Americas (SOA) Watch founded by Father Roy Bourgeois.

1992 Critical Mass (not an organization; it's an "unorganized coincidence") is founded to challenge the dominance of the car culture.

1992 Rage Against the Machine releases their self-titled first album.

48
THE DISABILITY RIGHTS MOVEMENT SAYS: "PISS ON PITY"

Thanks to activists from Lizzie Jennings to Rosa Parks, African-Americans can get on the bus...and sit anywhere they damn please. "Folks with disabilities," says Lucy Gwin, editor of *Mouth* magazine, "still can't get on the bus."

Newsflash to those who think Christopher Reeve represented the disability rights movement: The crips weren't impressed with Superman's search for a cure, they are not pacified by Jerry Lewis' telethons or legislation that is honored more in the breach, and they want freedom for the two million Americans imprisoned in nursing homes against their will. Now. Those are among the many reasons Gwin started *Mouth* and, as she puts it, "lowered the level of discourse on the subject of the helping system." As the crip mantra goes: "Nothing about us, without us."

"*Mouth* brings the conversation down to street level, where well-intentioned 'special' programs wreak havoc in the lives of ordinary people," Gwin says. "People talk about calling a spade a spade. We call Jack Kevorkian a serial killer. And when maggots outnumber nurses' aides at what others call a 'care facility,' we call it a hellhole. We say it out loud: if special education is so darned special, every kid in every school ought to have the benefit of it."

And don't get her started on the topic of mercy killing… or assisted suicide or whatever they're calling it these days. "Look at it this way: there are 53 million people with disabilities in the USA alone," Gwin states. "If we were so desperate to die, we'd be dropping off high buildings, hitting the pavement like rain. You'd have to climb over heaps of dead cripples to get to the bus stop in the morning."

"Individuals have a right to autonomy," Mary Johnson, editor of *The Ragged Edge*, told me. "If nondisabled people can kill themselves, then so should crips. But that's only part of the issue. The problem is this: If you did tell folks 'I'm going to kill myself' most likely everyone would try to get you not to do so. They'd get you counseling, get you help, but if a crip says 'I'm going to kill myself' they say 'Oh of course, we understand; we'll help.' See the double standard? It's the double standard that's the problem."

Another area of vexation is the lack of support and/or the inability to "get it" from progressive circles. From the movement's early days — The League of the Physically Handicapped was formed in New York City in May 1935 — right up to the current debates on Social Security and "right to die" issues, the Left has typically missed the opportunity to work collectively with those waging a crucial human rights battle.

"Disabled people's movements have much to add to the civilizing movements of the last three decades — the Civil Rights Movement, the women's movement and the gay and lesbian movement," says Marta Russell, author of *Beyond Ramps: Disability at the End of the Social Contract*. "It is disheartening, to say the least, when I can still pick up a book or read a call for unity to fight for social justice which omits or does not give equal weight to the disability social movement against oppression."

The situation is bleak… but don't even think about feeling sorry for anyone. As Marta, Lucy, Mary, and millions of others in the movement would tell you: *Piss on pity*. ☐

TIMELINE:

1993 Bill Hicks is banned by David Letterman.

1994 *Counterpunch* publishes its fist issue.

1994 Kurt Cobain commits suicide.

1995 William Blum writes *Killing Hope*.

1995 American Lori Berenson's imprisonment in Peru is widely protested.

1995 Ruckus Society is founded.

49
THE BATTLE IN SEATTLE

When activists made global headlines by essentially shutting down the meetings of the World Trade Organization in Seattle, Washington in November 1999, the term "anti-globalization" was bandied about without much serious explanation. The majority of those in the streets were not against the literal concept of global interaction… it was the current form of remote control imperialism euphemistically known as trade or globalization that inspired one of the most successful demonstrations in history.

"The WTO is an international organization… a forum for negotiating international trade agreements and the monitoring and regulating body for enforcing agreements," explains Michael Albert of *ZNet*. "The idea is simple," he adds. "Instead of only imposing on third world countries low wages and high pollution due to their weak or bought-off governments, why not weaken all governments and agencies that might defend workers, consumers, or the environment, not only in the third world, but everywhere?"

Created in 1995, the WTO is a bonanza for corporate profit that slipped in under the public radar.

"Most of America slept right through the birth of this 134-nation organization," says Mark Weisbrot, Research Director of the Preamble Center, in Washington, D.C., "including many in Congress who voted to ratify U.S. membership. In the fall of 1994 Ralph Nader's Public Citizen offered $10,000 to any member of Congress that would read the 500-page treaty and answer ten simple questions to prove it. Senator Hank Brown of Colorado, a Republican who had voted for

NAFTA and planned to vote for the WTO, took the bet. He passed the quiz with a perfect score, collected the winnings (for a charity of his choice), and then proceeded to announce that having read the agreement, he felt compelled to vote against it."

Brown's vote was not enough. Thus, when the truth about the WTO eventually became more widely known, the only vote left was by raising hell. The organization's decision to hold its annual meeting in Seattle provided activists with the stage they needed to be heard by millions.

It wasn't perfect… or anything even close. Different factions within the protestors feuded over goals, issues, and tactics… and the more liberal marchers inexplicably joined the mainstream chorus in denouncing so-called anarchists for violent behavior. Even the corporate media recognized that paradox, with the *Los Angeles Times* stating: "Leaders of the peaceful demonstrations have lashed out at the anarchists, accusing them of undermining their anti-globalism (sic) message by breaking windows and destroying property. The anarchists in turn accused the Seattle protesters of protecting the same private-property interests that the WTO represents."

Infighting and compromises aside, those five days in Seattle injected American dissidents into an internationalist movement. In their book, *5 Days That Shook the World: Seattle and Beyond*, Jeffrey St. Clair and Alexander Cockburn declare that the "street warriors" who were "initially shunned and denounced by respectable 'inside strategists,' scorned by the press, gassed and bloodied by the cops and National Guard" were able to: shut down the opening ceremony; prevent President Bill Clinton from addressing the WTO delegates; get the corporate press to actually mention police brutality, and force the cancellation of closing ceremonies.

…YOU'RE NOT SUPPOSED TO KNOW

Chuck Munson of Infoshop has listed the many accomplishments of the movement, post-Seattle. These include the international Indymedia network; the return of a direct action, confrontational style of protest; putting organizations like the WTO, World Bank, and International Monetary Fund (IMF) under the microscope; establishing the Internet as an activist's most valuable tool of communication; and inspiring millions across the globe to put their passions into action.

"Ours is a worldwide guerilla war of publicity, harassment, obstructionism," write St. Clair and Cockburn. "It's nothing simple, like the 'Stop the War' slogan of the 1960s. Capitalism could stop that war and move on. American capitalism can't stop trade and survive on any terms it cares for."

As Michael Albert has articulated, the goal is to globalize equity not poverty, solidarity not anti-sociality, diversity not conformity, democracy not subordination, and ecological balance not suicidal rapaciousness… or, as Arundhati Roy explains: "In the present circumstances, I'd say that the only thing worth globalizing is dissent." ⛝

TIMELINE:

1996 Howard Lyman exposes Mad Cow Disease on Oprah.

1996 "Democracy Now" first airs on Pacifica Radio.

December 10, 1997 to December 18, 1999 Environmental activist Julia "Butterfly" Hill lives on a 200-foot-tall ancient redwood tree named "Luna."

1998 Jane Kay Holtz writes *Asphalt Nation*.

1998 Student activists from over 30 different schools form United Students Against Sweatshops (USAS).

50
FAMILIES OF 9/11 VICTIMS SAY "NO" TO REVENGE

Post-9/11, it was less popular than ever to voice opposition to U.S. government policy… and never was it more important. Perhaps no collective voice of dissent has been more profound than that of the families of 9/11 victims involved in the group Peaceful Tomorrows. Their mission statement reads as follows:

Peaceful Tomorrows is an organization founded by family members of those killed on September 11th who have united to turn our grief into action for peace. By developing and advocating nonviolent options and actions in the pursuit of justice, we hope to break the cycles of violence engendered by war and terrorism. Acknowledging our common experience with all people affected by violence throughout the world, we work to create a safer and more peaceful world for everyone.

One member of Peaceful Tomorrows is Jeremy Glick. His father, Barry, was a Port Authority worker who died in the September 11 attack on the World Trade Center. Not content with letting others speak for him or paint him with the broad brushes of patriotism and revenge, Glick co-authored a book, *Another World is Possible*, and on February 4, 2003, appeared as a guest on Fox News Channel's "The O'Reilly Factor." The show's host, Bill O'Reilly — notorious for his right-wing agenda and obnoxious manner — was particularly irate about Glick signing an anti-war advertisement that included this passage: "We too watched with shock the horrific events of September 11 ... we too mourned the thousands of innocent dead and shook our heads at the terrible scenes of carnage — even as we recalled similar scenes in Baghdad, Panama City, and a generation ago, Vietnam."

O'Reilly told Glick he was surprised he'd sign an ad that "equates the United States with the terrorists." O'Reilly added: "I was offended by that."

Nonplussed, Glick stood his ground: "Our current president now inherited a legacy from his father and inherited a political legacy that's responsible for training militarily, economically, and situating geopolitically the parties involved in the alleged assassination and the murder of my father and countless of thousands of others. So I don't see why it's surprising."

As Glick continued on his point about the U.S. funding and arming Islamic extremists in Afghanistan at the time of the Soviet invasion, O'Reilly fell back on boilerplate ripostes like, "You are mouthing a far left position that is a marginal position in this society, which you're entitled to." The host added: "I'm sure your beliefs are sincere, but what upsets me is I don't think your father would be approving of this."

Here is some what followed:

GLICK: Well, actually, my father thought that Bush's presidency was illegitimate.

O'REILLY: Maybe he did, but ...

GLICK: I also didn't think that Bush ...

O'REILLY: ... I don't think he'd be equating this country as a terrorist nation as you are.

GLICK: Well, I wasn't saying that it was necessarily like that.

O'REILLY: Yes, you are. You signed ...

GLICK: What I'm saying is ...

O'REILLY: ... this, and that absolutely said that.

GLICK: ... is that in — six months before the Soviet invasion in Afghanistan, starting in the Carter administration and continuing and escalating while Bush's father was head of the CIA, we recruited a hundred thousand radical mujahadeens to combat a democratic government in Afghanistan, the Turaki government.

O'REILLY: All right. I don't want to ...

GLICK: Maybe ...

O'REILLY: I don't want to debate world politics with you.

GLICK: Well, why not? This is about world politics.

O'REILLY: Because, No. 1, I don't really care what you think.

From there, O'Reilly told Glick: "Keep your mouth shut when you sit here exploiting those people," "You have a warped view of this world and a warped view of this country," "Man, I hope your mom isn't watching this," and "Shut up," before finally turning to the show's engineer and demanding: "Cut his mic."

In less than 15 minutes, the façade of national unity behind military aggression was shattered forever. By promoting goals such as "educating and raising the consciousness of the public on issues of war, peace, and the underlying causes of terrorism" as well as calling attention to "threats to civil liberties, human rights, and other freedoms in the U.S. as a consequence of war," Jeremy Glick, Peaceful Tomorrows, and others who lost loved ones on September 11, are exercising their freedom of speech and expression when it is most needed. ♻

TIMELINE:

February 15, 2003 Millions of Americans take part in a day of global anti-war protest.

2003 Gay marriages are performed in Massachusetts.

2005 Ward Churchill faces a right wing assault for a post-9/11 essay in which he characterizes some of the victims as "little Eichmanns."

REFERENCES

Thomas Paine. Paine, Thomas. *Common Sense*. Philadelphia: W. & T. Bradford, 1776.

Bill of Rights. Amendments 1-10 of the United States Constitution. Philadelphia, 1791.

Shays Rebellion. Davis, Kenneth C. *Don't Know Much About History: Everything You Need to Know about American History but Never Learned*. Avon Books, 1990. § Zinn, Howard. *A People's History of the United States, 1492-Present*. Harper Perennial, 1980, 1995.

Nat Turner. Davis, Kenneth C. *Don't Know Much About History: Everything You Need to Know about American History but Never Learned*. Avon Books, 1990.

The Seminole-African Alliance. Katz, William Loren. "Christmas Eve Resistance to the First US Occupation" From CounterPunch [http://www.counterpunch.org/katz12242004.html] 24 December 2004. § Katz, William Loren. *Black Indians*. Simon Pulse, 1997.

Lowell Mill Girls Gets Organized. Flanagan, Alice K. *The Lowell Mill Girls (We the People)* Compass Point Books, 2005. § Dietch, Joanne Weisman, ed. *The Lowell Mill Girls: Life in the Factory (Perspectives on History Series)* Discovery Enterprises, Limited, 1998.

St. Patrick's Battalion. O'Connor, Anne-Marie. "Mexico, Ireland Share the Bond of an Ill-Fated Army" *Los Angeles Times*, 16 September 1997. § Ryal Miller, Robert. *Shamrock And Sword: The St. Patrick's Battalion in the U.S.-Mexican War.* University of Oklahoma Press, 1989. § Acuña, Rodolfo, *Occupied America: A History of Chicanos, 5th Edition.* Longman, 2003. § Stevens, Peter F. *The Rogue's March.* Potomac Books, 2005.

Thoreau. Thoreau, Henry David. *On The Duty of Civil Disobedience.* Massachussetts, 1849.

Uncle Tom's Cabin. Beecher Stowe, Harriet. *Uncle Tom's Cabin.* Jewett Publising, 1852. Beecher Stowe, Harriet. *A Key to Uncle Tom's Cabin.* Boston, 1853. § Shenkman, Richard. *Legends, Lies and Cherished Myths About American History.* Perennial, 1992.

Lizzie Gets On the Bus. Williams, Jasmin K. "I will not be moved." In *New York Post*; available on-line [http://www.nypost.com/learncenter/cextra/030404/class.htm] 4 March 2004.

Coxey's Army. Schwantes, Carlos A. *Coxey's Army: An American Odyssey.* University of Nebraska Press, 1985.

REFERENCES

Ida M. Tarbell. Zinn, Howard. *A People's History of the United States, 1492-Present* Harper Perennial, 1980, 1995. § Steffens, Lincoln. *Tweed Days in St. Louis.* § Riis, Jacob. *How The Other Half Lives: Studies Among the Tenements of New York.* Penguin Classics, 1997. § Sinclair, Upton. *The Jungle: The Uncensored Original Edition.* See Sharp Press, 2003.

Emma Goldman. Goldman, Emma. *Living My Life. Vol. 1* and *Vol. 2.* Dover Publications, 1930.

Jack Johnson. Flatter, Ron. "Johnson Boxed, Lived on Own Terms." From ESPN.com [http://espn.go.com/sportscentury/features/00014275.html]. § Zirin, Dave. "Hitting Back Against Racism: The Legacy of Jack Johnson" [http://www.counterpunch.org/zirin01142005.html] 14 January 2005.

Helen Keller. Rosenthal, Sally. "A Woman of Her Time—and Ours" Rev. of Dorothy Hermann's *Helen Keller: A Life.* In *Ragged Edge Magazine,* Jan/Feb 1999. § The Helen Keller Archive; available on-line [http://www.marxists.org/reference/archive/keller-helen/].

Eugene V. Debs. "The Espionage Act of 1917" in U.S. Constitution [http://www.usconstitution.com/EspionageAct.htm]. § Tussey, Jean Y. *Eugene V. Debs: Speaks.* Pathfinder Press; Reissue edition, 1994.

Katherine Hepburn. Berg, A. Scott. *Kate Remembered*. Putnam Publishing Group, 2003. Hepburn, Katherine. *Me: Stories of My Life*. Ballantine Books; Reissue edition, 1996.

The Bonus Army. Davis, Kenneth C. *Don't Know Much About History: Everything You Need to Know about American History but Never Learned*. Avon Books, 1990.

Strange Fruit. Atapattu, Don. "Songs of Protest and Peace: A Guide to Protest Music, Part One." From *Counter Punch* [http://www.counterpunch.org/atapattu02012003.html], 1 February 2003.

This Land Is Your Land. Guthrie, Woody. "This Land is Your Land: The Asch Recordings." Original Release Date: 18 February 1997. Label: Smithsonian Folkways. § Guthrie, Woody. *Bound For Glory*. Plume Books; Reissue edition, 1995.

Dorothea Lang. Library of Congress reference? § Phillips, Richard. "To Make the World a Place For Creation." Rev. of Lange Exhibit at the Art Gallery of New South Wales [http://www.wsws.org/arts/1998/mar1998/lang-m21.shtml] 20 March 1998.

REFERENCES

Charlie Parker. Marshall, Marilyn. "The real Charlie Parker: what the movie didn't tell you. (Clint Eastwood's movie 'Bird')," in *Ebony*, 1 January 1989. § Russell, Ross. *Bird Lives!: The High Life and Hard Times of Charlie (Yardbird) Parker.* Da Capo Press, 1996.

Brando. Seiler, Andy. "Brando remembered as brilliant, bizarre." For *USA Today*, available on-line [http://www.usatoday.com/life/people/2004-07-02-marlon-obit_x.htm] 7 February 2004. § Bosworth, Patricia. *Marlon Brando.* Viking , 2001.

Lester Rodney. Silber, Irwin, and Lester Rodney. *Press Box Red: The Story of Lester Rodney, the Communist Who Helped Break the Color Line in American Sports* Temple University Press, 2003. § Rampersad, Arnold. *Jackie Robinson: A Biography*. Ballantine Books, 1998.

Jackson Pollock. Solomon, Deborah. *Jackson Pollock: A Biography*. Cooper Square Press, 2001.

Salt of the Earth. Tony Pecinovsky. "Making a movie against all odds." Rev. of *The Suppression of Salt of the Earth: How Hollywood, Big Labor, and Politicians Blacklisted a Movie in Cold War America*, by James L. Lorence. In *People's Weekly World*, available on-line [http://www.pww.org/article/view/3599/1/167/] 14 June 2003.

I. F. Stone. Stone, I.F. *The Trial of Socrates*. Anchor, 1989.

Lolita Lebron. Roig-Franzia, Manuel. "A Terrorist in the House." *The Washington Post Magazine*, 22 February 2004.

Rachel Carson. Henricksson, John. *Rachel Carson: the environmental movement*. Millbrook Press, 1991. § Carson, Rachel. *The Silent Spring*. Mariner Books; 40th Anniversary edition, 2002.

Betty Friedan. Friedan, Betty. *The Feminine Mystique*. W.W. Norton & Co., 2001.
§ Davis, Kenneth C. *Don't Know Much About History: Everything You Need to Know about American History but Never Learned*. New York: Avon Books, 1990.

Ralph Nader. Croft, Karen. "Citizen Nader" at *Salon.com* [http://dir.salon.com/bc/1999/01/26bc.html]. 26 January 1999. § Nader, Ralph. *The Ralph Nader Reader*. Seven Stories Press, 2000.

Burroughs. Burroughs, William S., and James Grauerholz and Barry Miles, eds. *Naked Lunch: The Restored Text*. Grove Press, 2004.

REFERENCES

Lenny Bruce. Bruce, Lenny. *Lenny Bruce: An Autobiography: How to Talk Dirty and Influence People.* AMS Press, 1965.

Muhammad Ali. Zirin, Dave. *International Socialist Review* Issue 33, "Revolt of the Black athlete: The hidden history of Muhammad Ali" [http://www.isreview.org/issues/33/muhammadali.shtml] January–February 2004.

Cesar Chavez. Goodwin, David. *César Chávez: la esperanza para el pueblo. = César Chávez : Hope for the people.* David Goodwin; Spanish text translated by María Teresa Gonzáles, Marie Bisby and Marie Cabrol. Silver Burdett Ginn, 1991. § Grossman, Marc. From *Stone Soup*; available on-line [http://www.soup4world.com/thebook/heroofthemonth.html].

Hugh Thompson. In *Wikipedia Encyclopedia*, available on-line at [http://en.wikipedia.org/wiki/My_Lai].

American Indians and Alcatraz. Winton, Ben "Alcatraz, Indian Land." In *Native Peoples Magazine*, Fall 1999. Reprint available on-line [http://siouxme.com/lodge/alcatraz_np.html].

Tommie Smith and John Carlos. Zirin, Dave. "An Interview with John Carlos." *Z-Magazine*, December 2003 [http://zmagsite.zmag.org/Dec2003/zirin1203.html].

Stonewall. Carter, David. *Stonewall: The Riots That Sparked the Gay Revolution*, St. Martin's Press, 2004.

Angela Davis. Davis, Angela Yvonne. *Angela Davis: An Autobiography*. International Publishers; Reprint edition,1989.

Curt Flood. Flood Curt. *The Way It Is*. Trident Press, 1971.

Daniel Ellsberg. Franklin, H. Bruce. "Pentagon Papers Chase." In *The Nation*, 9 July 2001.

Charles Bukowski. Chivani, Anis. "The Life of a Bum: Against the Work Ethic." From [http://www.counter-punch.org/shivani0925.html] 25 September 2002. § Booth, William. "Charles Bukowski, Bard of Booze." In *The Washington Post*,. Available on-line [http://www.washingtonpost.com/wp-dyn/articles/A29917-2004Jul5.html] 6 July 2004.

Patti Smith. Bockris, Victor. *Patti Smith: An Unauthorized Biography*. Simon & Schuster, 1999.

Keith McHenry. Butler, C.T., Keith McHenry and Howard Zinn. *Food Not Bombs.* See Sharp Press, 2000.

...YOU'RE NOT
SUPPOSED TO KNOW

REFERENCES

John Robbins. Robbins, John. *Diet for a New America*. HJ Kramer, 1998.

Public Enemy. Warrell, Laura K. "Fight the Power." Available at *Salon.com* [http://www.salon.com/ent/masterpiece/2002/06/03/fight_the_power/]. 3 June 2003. § Nelson, George. *Hip Hop America*. Penguin, 1999.

Disability Rights. www.mouthmag.com. § Gwin, Lucy. "Postcards from the Planet of the Freaks." Article in *Everything You Know Is Wrong: The Disinformation Guide to Secrets and Lies*. Russ Kick, ed. The Disinformation Company: 2002.

Seattle. Albert, Michael. "A Q&A on the WTO, IMF, World Bank, and Activism." Available on-line [http://www.zmag.org/ZMag/articles/jan2000albert.htm]. § St. Clair, Jeffrey and Alexander Cockburn. *5 Days That Shook the World: Seattle and Beyond*. Verso, 2001.

9/11. www.peacefultomorrows.org

ABOUT THE AUTHOR

A self-educated kickboxing instructor who lectures on foreign policy at MIT in his spare time, *Newsday* calls Mickey Z a "professional iconoclast." *Time Out New York* says he's a "political provocateur." To Howard Zinn, he's "iconoclastic and bold." The author of four previous books, most recently *The Seven Deadly Spins: Exposing the Lies Behind War Propaganda*, Mickey lives in Astoria, New York with his wife Michele.

Acknowledgements

First and foremost, I'd like to thank Gary Baddeley and Richard Metzger for asking me to write this book and giving me such an opportunity... and a nod of gratitude to everyone at Disinformation who helped out and has been supportive of me over the years (Russ Kick, Alex Burns, Jason Louv, Ralph Bernardo, and Anne Sullivan to name just five). Also to Nick Mamatas for introducing my work to Disinformation, and Liz Lawler for compiling the references for this book.

My deep appreciation to the Puffin Foundation for their support in this project.

Thanks to Josh Frank, Greg Elich, and Mark Hand for input on content. To Howard Zinn, Dave Zirin, Kenneth Davis, and countless others for laying the groundwork. To Nancy Ryan for her tireless website support. To Winnette Glasgow, Harry MacDougal, and my cousin Sean Cullinan for computer-related help. To Mrs. Flood (my best high school writing teacher), my agent Claudia Menza, and of course, my incomparable parents.

Lastly, to Ariana and Joey: May you experience a more peaceful and just future.

EVERYTHING YOU KNOW IS WRONG
The Disinformation Guide to Secrets and Lies
Edited by Russ Kick
Do you get the feeling that everything you know is wrong? You'll find hard, documented evidence including revelations never before published on the most powerful institutions and controversial topics in the world.
Oversized Softcover • Cultural Studies/Political Science & Government • 352 Pages
$24.95 ISBN 0-9713942-0-2

YOU ARE BEING LIED TO
The Disinformation Guide to Media Distortion, Historical Whitewashes and Cultural Myths
Edited by Russ Kick
This book proves that we are being lied to by those who should tell us the truth: the government, the media, corporations, organized religion, and others who want to keep the truth from us.
Oversized Softcover • Cultural Studies/ Political Science & Government • 400 Pages
$24.95 ISBN 0-96641007-6

ABUSE YOUR ILLUSIONS
The Disinformation Guide to Media Mirages and Establishment Lies
Edited by Russ Kick
A stunning line-up of investigative reporters, media critics, independent researchers, academics, ex-government agents and others blow away the smoke and smash the mirrors that keep us confused and misinformed.
Oversized Softcover • Cultural Studies / Political Science & Government • 360 Pages
$24.95 ISBN 0-9713942-4-5

50 THINGS YOU'RE NOT SUPPOSED TO KNOW
By Russ Kick
Russ Kick has proved himself a master at uncovering facts that "they" would prefer you never hear about: government cover-ups, scientific scams, corporate crimes, medical malfeasance, media manipulation and other knock-your-socks-off secrets and lies.
Trade Paperback • Social Science / Popular Culture • 128 Pages
$9.95 ISBN 0-9713942-8-8

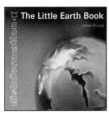

THE LITTLE EARTH BOOK
By James Bruges
The Earth is now desperately vulnerable; and so are we. This gift-priced-and-sized book contains stimulating mini-essays about what is going wrong with our planet and about the greatest challenge of our century: How to save the Earth for us all.

Paperback • Environmental Studies / Political Science & Government • 192 Pages
$9.95   ISBN 0-9729529-2-6

THE LITTLE FOOD BOOK
You Are What You Eat
By Craig Sams
Could the food we're eating be harmful to us? *The Little Food Book* tackles the issues on our own plates —those affecting the food we eat: genetic modification, farming subsidies, obesity and many others.

Trade Paperback • Environmental Studies / Health & Fitness • 160 Pages
$9.95   ISBN 1-932857-03-6

50 FACTS THAT SHOULD CHANGE THE WORLD
By Jessica Williams
This book is a series of snapshots of life in the 21st century. From the inequalities and absurdities of the so-called developed world to the vast scale of suffering wreaked by war, famine and AIDS in developing countries, it paints a picture of incredible contrasts. These are the facts YOU need to know.

Trade Paperback • Current Affairs / Popular Culture • 352 Pages
$14.95   ISBN 0-9729529-6-9

50 THINGS YOU'RE NOT SUPPOSED TO KNOW – VOLUME 2
By Russ Kick
Russ Kick delivers a second round of stunning information, forgotten facts and hidden history. Filled with facts, illustrations, and graphic evidence of lies and misrepresentations, *Volume 2* presents the vital, often omitted details on various subjects excised from your school-books and nightly news reports.

Trade Paperback • Popular Culture / Current Affairs • 144 Pages
$9.95   ISBN 1-932857-02-8

NOTES